Think on these Things

A series of devotional essays by **Rev. Canon S. E. Long**,
based on those written for the Orange Standard newspaper over several years.

Edited by **Dr. David Hume**

Published by the **Grand Orange Lodge of Ireland**, Belfast, 2006

I stay convinced that a good Orangeman is a good Christian man with a good influence on family, church and community. He is a man of standing, of exemplary character and conduct, respectful of all others and deserving of their respect. If this appears to be idealistic it is seeing things as they should be. We must be striving always to make the ideal the reality.

Canon S. E. Long

The Author

The Rev. Canon Dr. S. Ernest Long L. Th., M. Th., Th. D., D. Min, J.P. is a Grand Chaplain of the Grand Orange Lodge of Ireland, Honorary Vice President of the Imperial Orange Council, Honorary Grand Chaplain of Canada, and Hon. Deputy Grand Master of the Grand Lodge of the United States of America. He is co-founder and has been Worshipful Master of the Loyal Orange Lodge of Research No. 1994 and a member of Star of Down LOL No. 428 since the 1950s. He was the founder of "The Twelfth" magazine and of the Orange Standard newspaper, of which he remains a regular contributor, and of the Orange Torch (Scotland) and Orange News (New Zealand). He wrote an Ulster Scene article in the Sentinel (Canada) and the Sentinel (Australia) for many years.

A Church of Ireland clergyman, now retired, he lives in Belfast. He is a prolific writer and author of books, essays, papers, profiles, and pamphlets. This collection of devotional essays are among those which have been written by Canon Long for the Orange Standard newspaper over several years.

Publications by S. E. Long

Orangeism: A New Historical Appreciation (with Dewer and Brown)
The Orange Institution
Orangeism in Northern Ireland
Man for Ulster: Carson
The Orange Institution in the United States of America
The Parish of Dromara
W. P. Nicholson
William Shaw Kerr
The Clerical Presence in Orangeism
Three Courageous Churchmen
The emergence of Presbyterianism in Post Plantation Ulster
A Short History of the Church of Ireland
Rather be an Ulsterman
Dromara True Blues LOL No. 12
Beginning and Continuance (Lodge of Research No. 1994, paper)

LOOKING BACK: PLEASURE AND PROFIT

"Childhood shows the man." Milton

"Oh, when I was a tiny boy
My days and nights were full of joy
My mates were blithe and kind.
No wonder that I sometimes sigh
And dash the teardrop from my eye
To cast a look behind." Hood

There is always a beginning. Mine was in Burnaby Street, Grosvenor Road, Belfast, where my parents had lived for a few years, having moved from Spring Street, Woodstock Road, near to the Willowfield Church in which they were married. The move from East to West Belfast was to accommodate my father – a fitter at Coombe Barbour's Foundry, in Conway Street, between the Falls and Shankill Roads.

First generation city dwellers, he was from Magheramorne, near Larne, and she from Kells, both in Co Antrim. They were a good partnership, a blend of opposites, the calm and the fiery. Samuel was the original quiet man, thoughtful and earnest, Margaret outspoken, abrasive, determined that her way was best. He and we – two sisters and a brother – were under her command which was generally kind, generous, and defensive in its care of us.

Because my parents loved and respected one another and struggled together in the building of home and family in "The Hungry Thirties" they made a happy home for all of us. In common with all the men of his trade in these depression years my father had bouts of unemployment. It was a calamitous condition for someone to whom work was a physical and mental necessity.

School was nearby – St Philip's in Excise Street, "the wee school with the big master." It was Hugh Campbell who encouraged me to be a writer, and the teachers were Miss Johnston, Miss Gray and Miss Reid. I remember them respectively as placid, precise and pugnacious. The school was famed for its concentration on The Three Rs – reading, 'riting and 'rithmetic. It won prizes for the quality of its work. A major one was the Blue Riband.

Schools then were strong on discipline. Punishment was meted out, as I recall, sparingly, though frequent offenders were made to feel pain on hand or bottom.

Neither teachers nor pupils were bothered about a practice that was regarded as being justified, because it often had the desired effect on those foolish enough to disobey the rules.

Discipline in the home was of similar kind, for there the hand, or some easily reached instrument of correction, was used to compel obedience to a parental command. In my case punishment was administered by mum and she was a most able performer.

Our wee school had no space for recreations. The playing field was the street and there the boys played football, someone described it as chasing a ball and being chased by the police, for ball games were prohibited in the streets. This was not because of the traffic, it was very light, but on the complaints of adults without children and parents who feared having to replace broken windows. The girls, of course, had their own games.

The making of one's entertainment was essential, for these were the days when radio was little used and television was unknown. Everyone walked, for while there was a tram or bus available money was scarce and there were not the hazards of traffic and muggers. We walked everywhere, and there was climbing, too, for the Divis and Black Mountains were there to tempt us. But most of our adventures, and misadventures, were on the Blackstaff River which flowed via the Bog Meadows to the Belfast Lough bye-passing the football grounds of Linfield, Belfast Celtic, Broadway United and Distillery.

We played our soccer on Gribby's field, a little grassy patch beside the river and sometimes on the piece of waste ground on the other side of the Blackstaff at Milner Street. Years later after I visited the sites of our thrilling soccer matches I wrote an article, "Do you suffer from shrinkage?" What I had regarded, through the eyes of a child, as sizable was little larger than someone's front garden.

Not long after starting school I joined the Life Boys, the then-named kindergarten section of the Boys Brigade. We enjoyed games, competitions and physical exercises. When old enough for the B.B. proper, I was introduced to drill in fours, with intricate movements long since abandoned with the introduction of threes. I was encouraged by the Bible Class to recognise my need of a deep devotion to Christ and the Church. Our indebtedness to B.B. cannot be overstated. For me there was Sunday School in Excise Street School under the auspices of our Parish Church of St Philip, otherwise Drew Memorial. The teacher, I remember, was John Burns, a Harland and Wolff foreman iron moulder. His lasting interest in me meant that occasionally, for several years, he would appear at a service in which I was the preacher.

My mother was somewhat abashed when seven years old at a Sunday School party I "proposed a toast" to "Mr Eager, and his dishwasher." He was the Curate of the Parish. Another Curate of later date was T.J. Gray whose must memorable saying was to clergymen leaving their parishes, "you should never hold on to the tram after you jump off."

A disagreement between my mother and the Sunday School Superintendent over prizes had me transferred to Albert Street Presbyterian Church Sunday School in Percy Street, Lower Falls. My chum there and for the years into manhood was Jack Kelly. The teachers I recall were Wallace McCreery, a well known soloist and chorister, who enthralled audiences with his magnificent tenor voice of remarkable range, depth and strength. Most regrettably he died young, a grievous loss to the many who knew and loved him. Eric Barr was a thoughtful, kindly young man whose strengths as a teacher were his winsome manner and sense of humour.

Looking back I recall certain characteristics of those days, like neighbourliness. In times when many were semi-literate there was always someone to write their letters, and to provide practical advice to those who lacked confidence in their ability to express themselves well enough to obtain a positive result. One of these was Tommy Williamson, Excise Street, who had earned a reputation for his success in writing the kind of letters which got people jobs. He helped to solve marital problems and to keep some youngsters out of mischief. He had a neighbour a ready wit, who made responses like these: when a beggar at his door asked him for six pence for his bed he told him "bring it up the back till I have a look at it." He advised a workman slating on his roof, "Mister, don't come down that ladder for I've taken it away."

Some of my most exciting childhood experiences were in playing B.B. football. Our company, the 4th Belfast, was a small one but we had a few good players, among them Victor and Ernie Dawson. They were not averse to "edging the boot", that is being rough in the tackle. They were at it in Victoria Park when we played an East Belfast company there. When the game ended we had to grab our togs and flee from irate spectators, kin no doubt of players whom they felt were ill done by.

Our playing conditions were diabolical. Often the pitches were water logged or mud bound and the result of a match depended on the strength and durability of the players, for soccer skill was valueless. A pleasure we had was washing off the mud in a fast flowing, icy, stream in Falls Park. Dressing room facilities, when they existed, were primitive in the extreme everywhere. It was in Falls Park that one of our team was red-carded, the modern equivalent of "Sorry, son, you're off." Pa Bell, an officer of the BB FA, the substitute referee (for the man appointed hadn't shown up), was so kind a man that on the impassioned pleas of both teams Bobbie Ferguson was allowed to play on.

A fact of life is that we quickly grow, and go away from the companions of our childhood, and before I had reached manhood I had lost touch with nearly all of them. In those days there was a sharing and caring among people whose lives were church and community orientated and their interests localised. It was a time when travelling for work and play was limited and holidays were spent - if they were taken - in Bangor, though Newcastle and Portrush were popular. Day trips were generally as much as people could afford. We spent holidays in Bangor. We had relations there – my mother's sister, Rachel, was married to a Bangorian, Joe O'Neill, a railway signalman and racing pigeon fancier. Their family were our holiday companions.

I spent several childhood holidays in Magheramorne where I enjoyed the hospitality of another sister of my mother, Sarah, who was married to a brother of my father. He was William and his daughter, Isa, and son, Willie, were my close companions. I liked the country then and loved it for the thirty years of my ministry in rural Co Down.

Childhood and school days come to an end very quickly. At that time most youngsters were given no opportunity for educational advancement, and school leaving age for many was fourteen. The more fortunate boys got lengthy badly paid apprenticeships and girls had jobs in shops, offices, factories and mills and were often treated abominably.

The revolutionary changes in education and employment opportunities down the years has meant that the children of labourers and tradesmen got the chances denied their parents to enable them to earn their places in the professions, and as executives in industry and commerce, are well paid and affluent in how and where they live. So much has changed for the good for so many that it is inexcusable now to have deprived people among us. Yet there are those whose restricted education and training, lack of opportunities for gainful employment and recreational activities, militate against them. These are primary causes of much of the trouble in our society.

A regrettable difference from those other days is the strength of sectarianism which increasingly torments the country. We had no problem with Roman Catholic and Protestant relations. It held no danger for us to walk from the Grosvenor Road through McDonald Street to Albert Street and Church or Percy Street and Sunday School, or for my father to walk via Raglan Street to his workplace across the Falls.

While districts predominantly Roman Catholic and Protestant were recognisable, antipathies were largely absent. All that changed with 1969 and the years of terrorism which followed. The irony of life is that while the standard of living for the people is hugely improved, the struggle continues for peaceful co-existence in a place where people could live happily together, whatever their religious registration or political preference. It is the tragedy of this country that we failed to retain everywhere that sharing across the divides which marked our respect and concern for one another.

Remembrances may be enjoyable but always there is the regret that while we have gained so much with the changes time has brought we have lost values which must be rediscovered if we are to attain that maturity so admirable in good people and so necessary in a good society.

The Years Between

Jobs in the 1930s were very scarce, and what was available greatly restricted choice. The boys were often compelled to serve an apprenticeship to a trade in days when mills, factories and foundries, with the shipyard, were the main places of employment. Not by choice I became an apprentice iron-moulder in Coombe Barbour's Foundry, where my father was employed as a fitter. I look back on that time, spent in atrocious working conditions as a toughening up of life for me. The trade had been so neglected that craftsmen were compelled to use equipment, and methods that were outdated and labour intensive, which demanded a physical strength, which would have been unnecessary if production methods had been different and better.

Because of these problems there were many moulders and apprentices, most of them from the Shankill with the few from the Falls. The foundry was sited in Conway Street between the two roads which were Protestant and Roman Catholic enclaves. I do not recall any serious antagonism, the one with the other at this time. I can picture a few characters from those far off days – Jimmy Graham whose one subject was betting on horses; Billy Kennedy, the wild man out from work, drunken and quarrelsome, and in work a friend to his friends and a loud mouthed critic of his enemies, but who spent his weekends feeding the birds and animals in the Belfast Zoo; George Jefferson, a happy hearted Christian whose conduct was a practical testimony to his faith; and Billy Feeney, who said if he won the sweep he would go and see half of the world. When asked why not the whole world he replied, "There's half of it I would not want to see," and he gave his reasons. Living where I did I saw nothing of my workmates after hours, so that my friends were employed in various occupations.

Much of my free time was spent in organisational activities with the Boy's Brigade drill nights and football on Saturdays, and as a member of the Roden Street City Mission Hall, regularly it was Church on Sunday mornings and the mission hall at night. The fellowship of the hall was very good, and my chum Jack Kelly and I, were encouraged to teach in Sunday School and to speak at services. The missionary, David Forbes, was a W.P. Nicholson convert of the Twenties, a skilled and enthusiastic preacher and a fine singer. The war had him in France with the Army Scripture Readers, and after that overseas service, he was back with the City Mission briefly before going off to Canada with other Belfast City Missionaries to be Ministers in the Presbyterian Church there, but changed conditions of entry to that church prevented him being received and ordained in it. He became a Baptist Pastor. Influential among his mission colleagues he encouraged a few of them to follow him in ministry there. My indebtedness to the Roden Street fellowship is readily acknowledged. After Coombe Barbours I was employed in the Harland and Wolff Shadow Aircraft Factory, which was producing Sterling bombers for the R.A.F. A new and very much better environment made work more liveable than I had known it before.

The German blitzes on Belfast, however, meant that the factory was bombed and I moved to the King's Hall, Balmoral, which Short and Harland had taken over as part of their much larger aircraft business. I served there as a foreman and was responsible for the oversight of several tradesmen. The rebuilding of Harland and Wolff factory took me back there, and as a squad leader I had a team of some thirty tradesmen, and riveters who were often in need of special supervision. That meant keeping them on the job and to that task we seconded a less skilled tradesman with sergeant-major qualities.

My years in the aircraft industry were enjoyable, and profitable, for the wages were such that I was able to save money enough, with the addition of cash earned on vacations and in writing, to pay my way through college. Those were the days before grants for ministerial training.

I had tried, in the early days of the war, to enlist in the Crown Forces, but I was refused entry on the grounds that as an aircraft fitter in a reserved occupation I was of more value to the state in that job. In college, I found a few men whose situation had been the same as mine, but who were in receipt of sizable government grants. On enquiry from the Northern Ireland Minister of Education, Harry Midgley, I was advised that as all enlistments in Ireland had been voluntary I was not eligible, as they were, on that account.

I remain surprised that after the war, and my years in college in England, I was to meet up with only a few of my former workmates of the aircraft factories, when in the Ballymacarrett in which many of them had lived, was where I began my ministry in St Clement's Church, Templemore Avenue. It would appear that after the war and work being scarce many of them went off to work in Britain and beyond. None of them have been known to me for a very long time. Life is often compartmentised. We go through phases of life with their beginnings and endings, and as one door shuts another opens.

Always a reader, from childhood through youth to manhood, whatever else happened there was always the books. I was a cosmopolitan reader and the material I choose was always entertaining, enlightening and educational. The love of books meant that my studies were continuous over the years, and when serious and concentrated studies became necessary they were no hardship to me. Writing was always an enthusiasm of mine. I began to be published in the medium of access to would-be writers, "Ireland's Saturday Night," then a weekly magazine with articles and features of general interest, with a large content of sports reportage, commentary, results and analyses. I wrote about many things – incidents, events and people – and an early interest in pigeon keeping, homing and fancy, provided me with copy in the many aspects of the sport. I even published a booklet, "The Irish Pigeon Keeper," in 1944. Its publication got me a commission from the American fancy pigeon monthly, "The Pigeon Loft." It was edited by Professor Carl Naether, of the University of Southern California. I did a series of articles for the paper on Irish fanciers and their stocks and successes. And in my pre-college days I did some fifteen minutes talks on radio on racing pigeons. Those were the days when B.B.C. Northern Ireland had a Talks Studio with H G Fleet, John Boyd and John Body, with the producer Ursula Eason.

We had a writers circle with members who included well known contributors to the local papers and magazines here and elsewhere, among them Bill Murphy, Norman Harrison, Gerald Lyttle, Sam Napier and Desmond McIlroy. I recall as guest speakers well known literary figures like Joe Tomelty, Ruddick Millar and Harold Goldblatt.

I edited, without acknowledgement, the book by Jack Kilpatrick, "The Thoroughbred Racing Pigeon" which is still on sale after all these years. In "My Odyssey" published in "The Mourne Observer" and "The Church Magazine" and given as a lecture to a few societies I have a deal to say about my writing which has been very varied and comprehensive. I recall many friends who were especially near to me, and helpful to me in so many ways. Their portraits are safe in my bank of happy memories.

Fellow Travellers and Travel Guides

When we think on the way we have travelled we are reminded of our indebtedness to people who assisted us on the journey. We have been made as we are by how we thought and acted in the changes and challenges of life; and by the example and encouragement of others, what they said and how they influenced us as we met up with them on the way.

In my case there were many who had an influence on me to help me to face up to the challenges of life, character forming and destiny fulfilling in their effects. I owe my enthusiasm for the written word to my primary school principal, Hugh Campbell, "the big master in the wee school," St Philip's, Excise Street, Grosvenor Road, Belfast. He encouraged me to write when he displayed my "compositions" on the school notice board as examples of good writing and convinced me that I had the ability to write what others could read to their advantage.

There was my chum, Jack Kelly, whose devotion to Jesus Christ and pleasure in church going, so affected me that by deliberate decision, and in his company, I came to faith in Jesus. Together we began a spiritual pilgrimage that is traceable in its beginnings to Roden Street, Belfast City Mission Hall, when the missionary was David Forbes, a W.P. Nicholson convert, preacher and singer, and the encouragement we got there to learn and to teach the faith. Our faltering attempts at public speaking began there, and there I felt the pressure on me to "preach the gospel" as one ordained to ministry in the church. The studies, begun to that end, were interrupted for several years, by circumstances and experiences which governed my movements.

In the years in waiting there were those who helped me to keep the goal in sight. James Anderson was one of them. An elder in Albert Street Presbyterian Church we talked about how to proceed to that goal. It was he who obtained for me the practical assistance of the Rev. W.J. Gregg, the minister of Argyll Place Presbyterian Church, a most excellent scholar and pastor, who gave me, with a few others, a grounding in Old and New Testament studies and in the elementaries of Latin and Greek. I wrote about W.J. Gregg as "My Most Unforgettable Character." He exemplified the Christian graces of sincerity, honesty, sensitivity, humility and generosity. There, too was Betsy Sayers, who tutored me in Greek at her Cherryvalley home. I remember her for her good advice on studies. She was a member of that Methodist family that contributed so much to Methodism in Ireland. I recall when I was unhappy with my homework her saying, "You have done your best, don't argue with yourself."

In 1945 war ended and my job in the Harland and Wolff Aircraft Factory finished, I was in the position financially – there were no grants in those days - to study for the ministry. Studies at Shaftesbury House College, (Dr Renshaw's) prepared me for the Trinity College, Dublin, Entrance Examination. For personal reasons I chose to go to the London College of Divinity of which I had heard much that was likely to be of advantage to a mature student. F.D. Coggan was the principal, later to be successively Bishop of Bradford and Archbishop of York and of Canterbury. A most highly esteemed preacher, teacher and author, Dr Coggan was an exemplar for men, many of them just out of the Forces, to illustrate the necessity of a vocational commitment to ministry, holistic in its emphasis on the spiritual and the practical in life, and in the attitudes of pastor to people in whatever capacity he served them. On the college staff were men who earned high esteem as scholars, preachers, pastors and administrators, among them F.W. Dillistone, to become Dean of Liverpool, author and Residentiary Canon of St. Paul's Cathedral, London, R.S. Dean, later Bishop of Cariboo, Canada, Executive Officer of the Anglican Communion and Douglas Webster, author with a concentration on overseas missions, and to serve too, as a Residentiary Canon of St Paul's. Each of them made a lasting impression on me for personal qualities and characteristics worthy of emulation. William Shaw Kerr, Bishop of Down and Dromore, was not only agreeable to me training for ministry at LCD, but also took a lively interest in my studies there.

While I made many friends in college – I was elected soccer team captain and awarded a college Blue – I had a special friend, David Stephen. He and his wife had their home at Tooting, London, and I spent happy weekends there in my first year. David was born in Scotland, reared in Ireland and worked as a London City Missionary, and was annoyed, understandably, when he was described as a Welshman. His knowledge and experience of London was a mine of information on life and living there. Allied to an evangelical zeal in ministry these attributes set an example worthy of copying in selflessness and sacrifice for the cause of Christ.

My ordination was in St Clement's Church, Templemore Avenue, East Belfast, on 24 June 1949 by Bishop Kerr. Ordained with me were Warren Jones, Michael Dewar, Ross Jackson, Roy Cox, David Murphy and Jim Hall. Jim and I are the survivors of the seven. Ordained for St Clement's my Rector was W.H.N. Fisher. He was to serve in that capacity for more than forty years. Proud of his "blue blood", and a lover of literature and the spoken word – he was an orator and incomparable reader of the scriptures in church services and a practitioner of the pause in readings and prayers – he ministered happily in a parish where his extensive vocabulary was purposefully restricted to words and phrases "understood of the people".

At Willowfield, in my second curacy, the Rector was John Frazer, noted for his amazing ability to preach expository sermons using verse by verse of a scriptural passage, without notes and quotations perfect. And as a financier he ensured that his parishes were careful in their spending while encouraging them to be liberal in their giving to church and missions. A clergyman is advantaged if he has such a mathematical sense.

It was at Willowfield that I met a number of young men –they became my football team – who were to make me proud of them as churchmen and citizens. One of them was Gordon McMullan, who has had a notable ministry in the church as Pastor and Bishop, and whose scholarship has been recognised in Ireland and elsewhere in the world. If I had an influence on Gordon, and he says I had, he was to amply repay me when he encouraged me to obtain a university recognition of my literary work in several fields of study over very many years. The result was the production of three Theses for which I was awarded the degrees of M.Th., Th.D. and D. Min. My tutor was Jim Henry, Ph D., D.D., Congregational Minister, and highly regarded academic. His ability, and humility, endeared him to me and to the many who were much advantaged in our studies by the help of a sympathetic, sensitive and thorough teacher.

In my ministry there were so many who contributed to the sum of my knowledge and experiences that it would make a long list if I named them. I shall just thank most sincerely all those who journeyed with me for short or long lengths of my pilgrim's way. I was able on occasion by something I wrote, or what I said at thanksgiving services for someone's life, to express my indebtedness to them.

Colleagues who have been involved with me in my work can be assured that if they gained anything from knowing me they can be certain that I learned a great deal from knowing them. I must, however, mention especially Michael Dewar with whom I shared an interest and involvement in Orangeism. He and I wrote much and gained much from each other on what we wrote and how we talked together.

What I have said about people in church and other situations and how greatly I was indebted to them, I would repeat about the Orange Order.

I joined the Loyal Orange Institution as a Curate in St Clement's Church, and the Star of Down L.O.L. 428, when my Rector, Canon W.H.N. Fisher, was Chaplain. In 1950 the Lodge was one of the largest and most active in the then very big No. 6 District.

District Chaplain and then Deputy County Grand Chaplain of Belfast, I sat under the leadership of Canon Louis Crooks, a most gracious County Grand Master, and when Harry Burdge was a most competent and incisive County Grand Secretary. He had such a knack for anticipating questions that his responses to them, when they came, were such that he constantly amazed us with his encyclopaedia like knowledge of Orangeism and Unionism.

His fault to some was that he knew all the answers, and no secretary is expected to be so sure and confident of the certainty of what he said. He was succeeded by the amiable R.J. McMullan and Bishop Cyril Elliott was County Grand Chaplain.

In 1965 I was asked by a few members of the County Lodge who visited me at the Rectory, Dromara, to allow myself to be considered for the office of County Grand Master. When I was assured that the incumbent, John Bryans, would not stand again I consented on the understanding that if elected my tenure would be a short one. But at the election of Officers John Bryans was nominated; whatever other impression he had given my sponsors he was determined to carry on. He won by one vote. At the close of the meeting one District Master told me that had he known I was to be a candidate I would have had his vote but he had promised it, on his request, to John Bryans. Ironically one of the Brethren who had visited me at Dromara was absent, on some pretext, from the meeting. I was the first to congratulate John Bryans for, being a reluctant nominee, I was relieved with the result.

When he resigned as Grand Master of the Grand Orange Lodge of Ireland I was approached to stand for that office but I declined for three reasons – I would be unable to do justice to an office that required much time and travel; the wife and family would not want me to consider it; and I had the pastoral oversight of two parishes and as Rural Dean of some others, and with a large involvement in the committees of the Church of Ireland.

I was elected a Grand Chaplain over thirty years ago and Imperial Grand Chaplain at Toronto in 1982 and in 1994 in New Zealand, in my absence, I was appointed an Honorary Vice President of the Council. This body without executive powers is useful for the sharing of attitudes and experiences by Officers and Delegates in the several Orange Order jurisdictions. Regrettably many of those brethren whose friendship meant so much to me are no longer with us.

From the beginning my interest in and work for the Institution was as speaker, preacher and writer. I value most highly the influence and effect of the written word, for it only has permanence. "The Twelfth" magazine of the Belfast County was my idea, as was also "The Orange Standard". The first with Martin Smyth as co-editor and the second with Douglas Sloan, professional journalist and editor in that capacity.

My writings on the Institution, and for it, have been very many and publication of them has been in the several Orange jurisdictions. Writing continues to be a large part of my life. In spite of the years I still find much in Orangeism which is ever relevant religiously, ethically and politically.

I stay convinced that a good Orangeman is a good Christian man with a good influence on family, church and community. He is a man of standing, of exemplary character and conduct, respectful of all others and deserving of their respect. If this appears to be idealistic it is seeing things as they should be. We must be striving always to make the ideal the reality.

Section One:

Christ and the Christian:
Lessons from Life

The power of prayer

The call to prayer in times of national emergency is constantly being repeated in local situations where there is trouble and strife. The plea for divine intervention is understandable, for people pray instinctively when they are conscious of their own inability to solve their problems.

Some children recognised this for when a teacher asked the question: "What makes man distinct from other animals?" there were suggestions - worker, thinker, player, but when it was seen that the other animals also possessed these abilities the conclusion was that man is the one who prays.

"I assure you that whatever you ask the Father He will give you in My name. Up to now you have received nothing in My name; ask now, and you will receive that your joy may be overflowing." John 16:24

"Let prayer be the key of the morning and the bolt of the evening" said Matthew Henry.

But what is prayer? No definitions are more pithy and pertinent than these - it is the voice of faith; it is conversation with God. Those who pray regard it as the highest activity of which the human soul is capable. The people of the Bible who are featured prominently whatever their role in Biblical history are always men, and women, of prayer. Jesus is THE man of prayer. He spoke with certainty about its value, "Ask and you shall receive" and gave us the Pattern Prayer in which the proper relationship with God and concern for people is spelled out with brevity, sensitivity, selflessness and simplicity.

Prayer was the motivating force in the life Jesus lived in order to fulfil God's will and purpose for him. In all he said and did there was the sense that God was in everything with Him. Prayer was conversation with and instruction from God. As it was once described, "Prayer is not asking favours; it is asking for orders."

Prayer is real and effective but only when it is accepted that there are recognisable essentials in prayer - it is to God and for His help in every situation and circumstances of life. Because it is possible to pray aright it is possible to pray amiss. Prayer is ineffective when it is self-interested. We are assured that, "They never sought in vain who sought the Lord aright." (Robert Burns). There is the thought:

"To say my prayers is not to pray, Unless I mean the words I say; Unless I think to whom I speak, And in my heart His favour seek."

The point is made in the story Jesus told of the two men at prayer, a pharisee and a publican, the one self-centred and self-satisfied, the other in his humility could only pray, "God be merciful to me a sinner." Self-praise from one, penitence from the other. The prayer of one valueless, of the other necessary and valuable.

The effectiveness of prayer is accepted by those who pray as they are advised to do by Jesus himself. And we pray individually and collectively, for prayer is a major part of Christian worship. The essentials that apply to personal prayers are applicable to those of believers when they assemble together to worship their God.

The form of prayer is important to worshippers. The preferred prayers may be set and printed or of the moment. Christians often value well-ordered prayers to which an Amen can be readily given.

They see the prayers, hear, know, love and use them. And there are many who choose the spontaneity in prayer even when they are aware of the warning, "In extempore prayer, what men most admire God least regardeth" (Thomas Fuller). Whatever the preferences the essentials are to be recognised. To be avoided are prayers that are just words and worse when they are like that of the pharisee, a specimen of which was described as "The finest prayer ever offered to a Boston audience."

Tennyson on the effectivenss of prayer said:

"More things are wrought by prayer, Than this world dreams of. Wherever let thy voice Rise like a fountain to me night and day. For what are men better than sheep or goats if knowing God, they lift not hands of prayer, Both for themselves and those who call them friend."

Sarah Foulkes Moore judges that "every great movement of God in the world can be traced to a kneeling figure." Melanethon, the reformer, had this personal testimony; "Trouble and perplexity drive me to prayer, and prayer drives away perplexity and trouble."

The hallmarks of the Christian

The most compelling influence on the Christian should be the example of Jesus.

What He thought and taught, the quality and purpose of His life and the significance of His actions. For "Jesus is the pattern person upon whom the Christian must mould his life." St. Peter, in a memorable phrase, encouraged the first Christians to "walk in His steps." The thought conjured up the picture of the Christmasy Good King Wenseslas trudging through the deep snow with his little pageboy treading in his foot steps so that he could journey with him more safely.

The Christian has the advantage of having Jesus to lead him in the way he should go. His attitudes to God and life and living are to be the motivations of those who call themselves Christians.

SELFLESSNESS: The selflessness of Jesus is the reminder constantly that we are expected to be as He was in character and conduct. The qualities which endeared Him to others should be those that we show and that persuade people to see us as Christians in word and deed. The Christlikeness of Christians is effective in bringing individuals and communities to the knowledge of God and into the paths of righteousness.

St. Paul in Romans 15:1-6 provides us with what are the distinctive marks of the Christian, and of the Church

- consideration one for the other; common sharing to mutual advantage;
- the offering of everyone's abilities and talents for the progress of the faith;
- constant use of the Scriptures, God's ordinary means of communication with people.

The selflessness of Christians has brought much benefit to humanity in every facet of human thought and activity. The histories of many nations admit their indebtedness to Christians who copied Christ to provide standards of character and conduct and service to others which brought everlasting benefit to them. Too often, though, Christianity has not been well served by Christians who have displayed all the weaknesses, inefficiencies and ineffectiveness of their unChristlikeness. While the benefits of the faith have been brought by some, others have given it a bad name for all the reasons so roundly condemned by Jesus in the behaviour of religious men in the days of His flesh. It is a sad indictment on Christians when they are described as being very little different in attitudes and emotions to their non religious neighbours.

SCRIPTURES: Emphasis on the place and purpose of the Scriptures is always necessary for the book is not much used even by those deeply committed to the faith. The question was posed: "If God is a reality, and the soul is a reality, and you are an immortal being, what are you doing with your Bible shut?"

The message of the Bible is that God is and faith in Him is the one way to appreciate the fullness of life. A simple and practical use of the Scriptures is to rely on the promises of God to us.

Alexander Whyte, the Scottish preacher, started off each day, rhyming what he called his "promise text." He described how he "put them on his tongue and sucked them like a wee sweetie." He had many of them such as, "If God can be for us who can be against us." "My God shall supply all your need," and "Lo, I am with you always". An old jingle had it, "A verse a day keeps the devil at bay."

The Scriptures provide us with the priorities of Christ and the principles the Christian lives by - fortitude is needed, not the passive acceptance of whatever happens but making every experience of value for future use. C.H. Spurgeon said, "No one ever outgrows Scripture, the Book widens and deepens with the years."

EXPECTATION: St. Paul's fortitude had its basis in hope, the confidence that no matter how awful the situation it has an end and the promise of something better to come. He was never a pessimist. He had faced and lived through many terrifying experiences and was able to say: "I have been knocked down many times but I have never been knocked out." (1 Corinthians 11:16). The hope that allowed Paul to do great things for God was God inspired and God centred. He had no delusions about people even when he admired them for their goodness, generosity, courage, endurance and achievements. His dependence was on God and the knowledge that He would look after him.

FELLOWSHIP: St. Paul had things to say about the fellowship among believers, the harmony necessary for them to work together for Christ and Church and people. An original himself he would bind no one in a mental straight jacket of belief and practice. He recognised the special gifts and abilities of others and paid compliment to them in their work. The church is only being effective when it uses willingly whatever its members contribute to it. How they view their commitments to Christ and to the church is to be the governing factor in their relationships.

Differences should not be disruptive, not allowed to have a divisive effect on the fellowship.

The splintering of Christendom has been a grave disability in the work and witness of the church. Made even less justifiable by those who value themselves so highly that faith and fellowship are to be shared only with those who think and act as they do.

ENJOYMENT: St. Paul struck another note of praise to God, the joy of believing in Him and sharing it with fellow believers. The happy spirit is an attraction when joylessness is off-putting and repelling. We have to pose the question constantly, "How do I and my church compare with the patterns set for us by Christ and the first Christians?"

Mirth is God's message

"A sense of humour is the philosophy of the unbeaten."

Clergymen have always been good targets of the would-be occasional comic and of the professionals as well. They take the stories against themselves in good part. They recognise the therapeutic value of smiling often and laughing frequently. On occasion they retell the stories for they know that people enjoy the piece of nonsense which is forever in the good joke. After all they are among those who see life as it is - tragic and funny. "The web of our life is of mingled yarn, good and ill together."

Humourists are our benefactors for they soften with mirth the ragged inequalities of life. They have no respect for persons - the proud are inflated and the humble exalted.

They show people as they are in their weaknesses and strengths - their cruelties, hypocrisies and generosities.

There is, of course, the down side of a humour unworthy of the name for it is sacriligeous, malicious, racist and indecent. The best things in life are always in danger of being abused and misused. "Men show their character in nothing more clearly than by what they find laughable."

"The fun of the cloth" is that nonsense in which good humour is sometimes made to make people think of the serious which always shadows the frivolous. There is a subtilty in humour. It has a wisdom of its own.

Most clergy believe that "the laughter of people is the contentment of God."

Don Lewis's book "More Reverend Sirs, Ladies and Gentlemen" is a compilation of irreverent parables and light-hearted anecdotes. For example; a curate about to leave a parish for a charge of his own received a going away present of a silver tea service. In his thanks for the gift he began, "I will not call you ladies and gentlemen for I know you too well for that."

A vicar was so embarrassed when his curate became the love of the ladies of the parish that he asked him to seek another post. "No need," said the curate, "there is safety in Numbers." "That's were you're wrong," explained the vicar, "your only safety is in Exodus."

Dean Jonathan Swift visited the Three Crosses Inn where he found the landlady most offensive. Before he left he used his diamond to write on the window,

> *To the landlord. There hang three crosses at thy door, Hang up thy wife and she'll make four.*

At his marriage Bishop George Reindorp said: "My wife is a medical doctor, and I'm a doctor of divinity. So you might call ours a marriage of body and soul."

Announcements in church are commonplace. Occasionally, one raises a smile when it goes like this, "On Friday the Mother's Union will hold a jumble sale. This is a chance for all the ladies ..... to get rid of anything that is not worth keeping, but too good to be thrown away. Don't forget to bring your husbands."

Charles King Irwin, the former Church of Ireland Bishop of Connor, never wasted a word. He had a letter from a curate who wanted to change churches. He gave two lengthy reasons for his request. The reply was 1) No. 2) No.

Newport White, the church historian, accosted by a rude American looking for a certain place in the Shelbourne Hotel, Dublin, directed him. "Take that corridor, turn left at the bottom, you will see a door marked Gentlemen, don't let that deter you, that's the place."

Dean A.L. Myles, Tullylish, spoke of young clergy holding his hand and feeling his pulse. That reminds me of:

> *"A vicar, long ill, who had treasured up wealth. Told his curate each Sunday to pray for his health. Which oft having done, a parishioner said, that the curate ought rather to wish he were dead. 'By my troth,' said the curate, 'let credit be given I ne'er prayed for his death but I have for his living.'"*

It could have happened to a cleric who said, "I have lost my portmanteau

> *"I pity your grief. It contained all my sermons, I pity the thief."*

Curran, the Dublin barrister, told Father O'Leary: "I hope when I die you will have the key to heaven." "Why?" asked the priest, "Because if you had you'd let me in," explained Curran. "It would be easier for you," retorted O'Leary, "If I had the key of the other place, then I could let you out."

Another of the kind. The peacher's sermon was on Jonah and the Whale. After the service he was questioned by a cynic: "You don't really believe that story do you?" The preacher replied: "I have promised myself when I get to heaven I'll ask Jonah about it." "But what if he's not there?" persisted the cynic. "Then you can ask him," was the immediate response.

Before an infant baptism the minister was informed that the child was to be named, Alfred Homer. Intrigued, the minister asked, "Homer, is he your favourite Greek poet?" "Poet, never heard of him," said the father, "I keep homing pigeons."

Another cleric asked why the names were to be Alpha Omega had the mother's tight lipped response, "He's the first and the last."

When T.A.B. Smyth went to preach his trial sermon in Clougherny Presbyterian Church he arrived early and greeted the congregation, who, country fashion, were chatting outdoors before the service. His friendliness so impressed that one man made the comment: "It doesn't matter how he preaches he's the man for us." After the ordination and installation in the church an elderly minister on being introduced to him said, "So this is the young man who smiled his way into Clougherny."

Need we add that the best of jokes are often of the moment and the single incident, unexpected and unrehearsed.

The Seeking Mind

The Christian, being a disciple of Jesus, is a learner, a gatherer of knowledge about Him, His life and teaching and its influence on the lives of people. He seeks to share that knowledge. He takes in to give out. And the process is continuous, life long, for there is always more to know about God and more to see of the effects of faith in Him.

There is need then for an open mind, a willingness to be taught, to discover new things or to see old things from another perspective. We must beware of closed minds, of thinking that what we know is complete and sufficient.

Jesus encouraged people to think, to be seekers after truth about God and life and death. He used a teaching method, the story to persuade people to think their way through to knowledge; and to experience the benefits of a greater awareness of the world around them.

He condemned the Pharisees' who thought that all wisdom had been gathered up in their literature and law. They refused to open their minds and remained Pharisees, separated ones, separated from greater knowledge and final truth. Christians can be like that.

Yet the Christian faith is always growing and developing in its enveloping of its thinking on everything that affects humanity. God is always opening up new things to seeking minds.

He speaks to us through the Scriptures, which are His ordinary means of conversation with us. Bible reading is integral to Christian living, for the book has unfathomable riches. However much is taken from it there is always more available from a well that never dries up. The evangelist C.H. Spurgeon said, "Nobody ever outgrows Scripture, the book widens and deepens with our years."

This is because the Bible is the most thought-suggesting book. None other deals with such grand themes together. In it the unlearned may obtain all essential knowledge and the learned may discern their ignorance of much of what should be known. It is essential to let the Bible speak for itself; to read and study it for oneself. But sharing is of the essence of the faith and to share thought with others on what we read is beneficial to us. That is why we have daily Bible reading notes, Bible commentaries and Bible classes. It is the reason why in the worship of God we have a place for the reading and exposition of the Scriptures. The sermon is a preacher's thinking on a passage of the Bible and his task is to consider with his congregation the implications of what the Bible says on what matters to people. It is to the grievous loss of the church if "the preaching of the Word" is not treated as seriously as it should be. It is often by "the foolishness of preaching" that God speaks loudly, clearly and convincingly to people.

The church has been at its best when the emphasis has been on preaching and when by it people were brought to faith in Christ or strengthened in their faith in Him. It was ever so, for from the beginning the sermons of the Apostles produced growth in the church, and a greater and deeper devotion to Christ with more active witness to the value and purpose of Christian living. Preaching and prayer. Prayer is essential in the Christian's faith and life. It is in its several forms the means of contact, constant, continuous and effective with God. It is the voice of faith. The earthy Rabbie Burns thought: "They never sought in vain that sought the Lord aright." Paul advised people, "Don't worry over anything whatever; tell God every detail of your needs in earnest and thankful prayer and the peace of God, which transcends human understanding will keep your hearts and minds as they rest in Christ Jesus" (Philippians 4:8). Prayer is not eloquence but earnestness; the feeling of helplessness and the expectations of help from God to overcome one's difficulties. Abraham Lincoln was thinking about that when he said: "I have been driven many times to my knees, by the overwhelming conviction that I had nowhere else to go. My own wisdom, and that of all about me seemed insufficient for that day."

The need for self-control and discipline needs to be realised

"Do you remember how, on a racing track, every competitor runs, but only one wins the prize? Well you ought to run with your minds fixed on winning the prize. Every competitor in athletic events goes into serious training. Athletes will take tremendous pains - for a fading crown of leaves. But your contest is for an eternal crown that will never fade. I run the race with determination. I am no shadow boxer, I really fight. I am my body's sternest master for fear that when I have preached to others I should myself be disqualified." 1 Corinthians 9:24, 25.

It is accepted everywhere that athletic success is possible only if there is self-control; the self-discipline of the athletes, their utter devotion to the goal, to win the top prize. There has to be this incredible dedication from athletes in all the games and sports. Competition is so intense that in many of them total absorption of time and training is absolutely necessary.

This determination to reach the top has the constant reminder that success is dependent on pre-competition practice and coaching. Where there is not sufficient hard work victory is for others. Success can never be certain. It is possible with ability and the will to win.

The intention to reach the highest standard has to be the aim if there is to be success in anything worth doing.

There is danger, of course, in total commitment in any career or cause, work or sport. It can be selfish and repulsive. Participants need to recognise the place and worth of others who strive to obtain the same goal.

The emphasis these days is on self-expression, on people doing their own thing in their own way. Society puts the restriction by demanding that they control themselves as good citizens.

Most of us are taught in childhood to treat others unselfishly, to be kind to them and to expect the same treatment in return. We are taught to think before we speak, to be careful of what we say and how we say it and not to jump quickly to conclusions. All children should be taught to treat people and things respectfully and honestly, and to recognise their indebtedness to others like parents, friends, teachers and preachers. What they teach and what children learn from them is of permanent value.

We are better people when we are self controlled and determined to make the best of ourselves; to use well our opportunites to fulfil our potential and to grow in worth.

Our good intentions can be restricted, diverted, by the weaknesses of the flesh, laziness, thoughtlessness and self-devaluation. We may be prevented from fulfilling ourselves by these barriers in our way. It is never easy to overcome them but to do that is necessary for our well being.

Self-control is not irksome when it has purpose behind it. Paul the apostle was totally dedicated to Christ. His plan was in the statement, "I go straight for the goal - my reward the honour of being called by God in Christ." Phillippians 3:14.

Paul's total commitment brought him joy but also scourgings, shipwreck, loneliness and imprisonment. He felt that what he had to do and be was no burdensome task, for him the cause and the benefits made everything worthwhile. And there were always good friends and supporters to help him in every emergency, but above all the consciousness of the presence of Christ with him all the time.

The Christian is faced with two choices - to please himself or to live with the set purpose of serving Christ and other people. It has been said that the true calling of a Christian is not to do extraordinary things, but to do ordinary things extraordinarily well. Tasks of whatever kind can be done in a gentle, generous spirit that overrides all petty paltry feelings and elevates all that has to be done. There is always the example of Jesus.

The man on the cross

"We preach Christ crucified". 1 Cor. 1:23.

"We may not know, we cannot tell
what pains he had to bear,
But we believe it was for us,
He hung and suffered there."
Mrs. Alexander.

There is a picture titled "The Shadow of the Cross" by Holman Hunt. It shows the carpenter shop at Nazareth with Joseph and the boy Jesus at work. Jesus pauses, stretches himself, and his outstretched arms and erect body throw the shadow of a cross upon the wall of the shop. The study is fanciful: its message is true. It is hard to read the Gospels without concluding that His destiny was the Cross on Calvary's Hill. The New Testament says that the death of Jesus Christ was of paramount importance. His birth, wonderful as it was, marked the coming of God into the world in flesh and blood. His ministry, wonderful as it was, marked the beneficent activity of God in the lives of people. But His death possessed the greatest importance. "Our Lord came to earth for the express purpose of dying." (Griffith Thomas).

Most space in the Gospels is given to the passion and death of Jesus, that is so because His death is central in scripture, history and worship. It is clear from the accounts of the evangelists that the first disciples did not understand Jesus when He talked about His death, they failed to appreciate what He was saying to them. They refused to believe that a premature death would spell finis to such a promising, exciting and enthralling life, such were their expectations from their connections with Him. But Jesus was never in doubt. He knew what His end would be. Elizabeth Barratt Browning put these words into his mouth:

> *"As I shall be uplifted on a cross, In darkness of eclipse and anguish dread,*
> *So shall I lift up in my pierced hands, Not into dark but light - not unto*
> *death, But life - beyond the reach of guilt and grief, The whole creation".*

The reason He died was for us men and our salvation. He died as a criminal though He was guilty of no crime. He died voluntarily, "I lay down my life of myself". He could have saved it by speaking and acting differently. "He was constrained to die not by outward compulsion but by inward necessity." No two witnesses could be found to agree on a charge against Him. Pilate, the Governor, found Him faultless. Herod, the King, discovered nothing to His discredit. And Christians came to see Him as the great and final sacrifice for the sins of people. They believed with Peter, "He died the just for the unjust that He might bring us to God," "Who His own self bare our sins in His own body on the tree," and with Paul, "Christ died for our sins."

Christ's death was an atonement, bringing God and people together, making good a broken partnership. In World War One a signaller was sent out to repair a broken communications with headquarters at a crucial point in the battle. He did the job and the situation was saved but later the man was found beside the joined wires his hands in death binding them together. The action was Christ-like in its consequences.

In the New Testament the crucifixion of Jesus is described as an act of God. "God was in Christ personally reconcilling the world unto Himself." It was the love of God in action. "He loved me and gave Himself for me."

> "There was no other good enough to pay the price of sin, He only could unlock the gate of Heaven, and let us in."

He was the sacrifice, the means of bringing people into a proper relationship with God.

The sacrifices of the Old Testament were the means whereby God's people were brought closer to Him. The sacrifice of Christ meant that "God commended his love towards us in that while we were yet sinners Christ died for us." (Romans 5:8). The crucifixion and God's acceptance of the sacrifice of Christ restored the broken relationship, and the divine forgiveness is assured to all who seek it in faith and penitence.

Dr. David Smith explained the position: "Forgiveness is ours already by right and it becomes ours in actuality the moment we claim it."

The command of the Gospel is not believe and your sin will be forgiven, but your sin is forgiven believe and receive your heritage.

The sacrifice of Christ calls people to copy the selflessness He showed in His death. He said, "If anyone wishes to follow in My footsteps let him renounce self, take up his cross and follow Me." (Matthew 16:24). The atoning sacrifice of Christ is the essential truth of the Christian faith for "The Cross is the supreme manifestation of the love of God." (J.S. Whale) "The proof of God's amazing love is that Christ died for us." (Paul).

The church was born of the Cross and it exists to proclaim it in worship, fellowship and service to people. At the Cross we see God, our own humanity and the claims of God upon us. We may feel the need to live as Jesus did in dependence on God and know as He did the truth of "All from God, all for God."

The Christian Citizen

The first murderer named in the Bible asked the question, "Am I my brother's keeper?" with the implication that the answer had to be "no". Many people are like Cain in that they refuse to accept that they have responsibility in another's situation, be he brother, neighbour or fellow citizen. Some have made a virtue of "keeping myself to myself" and of living by the old adage "Minding my own business". This attitude can not be acceptable for Christians who are described as those who are members one of another. There is no denying common humanity and no questioning of the contention that everyone is valuable in the sight of God, those who are His in the fellowship of faith and those who are not.

Christians are committed to the principle of mutual sharing to mutual advantage. There is a primary responsibility to serve others as the servants of Christ, to be good citizens.

"Land of our birth we pledge to thee
Our love and toil in the years to be,
That we may hold from age to age
An undefiled heritage".

We do that by acknowledging the Biblical precept, "Righteousness exalteth a nation" and by living honest, honourable and good lives.

Normally the state takes no account of wrong doing until it becomes a punishable offense in law. But we know that behaviour which disregards the moral law has its ill effects in the sinner, his family and the community. No one can do wrong and not hurt somebody. The behaviour patterns of Christians must be much higher than the state demands. When they are true to their Christian commitments they live less for themselves than for others. They may not be like those who are frequent users of the personal and possessive pronouns, "I, me, my and mine". There is a reminder that the Cross of Christ is the personal pronoun crossed out.

People are often acquisitive. They have an insatiable appetite for things. They lay great store on their possessions or what their money can buy for them. Some are so ambitious and self-seeking that they must win their goals whatever the cost to themselves and to others. Many avoid the responsibilities of a citizenship which requires participation in the working and administration of their society. They will not be involved in community concerns even to the exercise of the franchise in elections. They ignore the fact that "bad public officials are appointed by good citizens who do not vote".

The fact that the state is what its citizens make it is a generality relevant in a democracy. And in a democracy people should be treated with respect regardless of differences, in age, sex, colour or race. It should want the good of all its people. Its standards should be those of its best people, the kind unselfish, generous citizens who lift up their humanity by their concern for and treatment of others who need their help. Gilbert Murray, drawing attention to the weaknesses, insecurities and inefficiencies of people, obseved, "Normally every government is possessed by a devil, the devil of the massed and organised selfishness of the nation".

Christians with their developed sense of responsibility for the well-being of the people have different standards and attitudes to those whose interests are selfish and care less of the circumstances of their fellow citizens.

There are recognisable principles for Christian citizenship in these propositions:

- Happiness lies more in giving than receiving.
- People are not separate units but intimately related to one another.
- The greatest among you must be your servants.
- This is God's world and God is love. Love is in caring for others.
- Someone with these in mind coined the phrase, "God first, others second, self last".

The constant rule of the Christian life is that we serve God in serving our fellowman to the pattern set by Jesus who went about doing good in the days of His flesh.

The Christian citizen doing the will of God seeks to improve the society in which he lives. God's will is always for the good of people.

Christian charity

"And if anyone gives as much as a cup of cold water to one of these little ones, because he is a disciple of Mine, this man will assuredly not go unrewarded".
Matthew 10:42.

The word charity has been often been misused and misunderstood. Some have been called charitable when they gave a little amount to a needy person or cause even when the gift made the giver superior and the receiver inferior.

Charity is the greatest of the three theological virtues and is the mark of that Christian care and concern which is outgoing to help others whatever their need. It is without self interest and ostentation. It is gratitude for the ability and the opportunity to be kind to those less fortunate than oneself. It has neither pride nor hypocrisy; just humility and generosity.

The Christian believes that what he has are God's gifts to him. Thankfulness to God requires him to care for others as God cares for him. It gives meaning to a relationship, "the brotherhood of man in the family of God". From the first Christians cared for one another to meet each others physical and material needs, there was always the recognition of the duty to do this or to ensure that means were available for this to be done.

While it has never been a matter of Christians only doing works of mercy and pity - those of other religions and none have shown similar concerns - they have been quick to respond to cries for help from those in distress whether near or far. Many of those who earned gratitude for their charity and charitable foundations were motivated by their Christian commitment. St.Basil explains: "I have learned from Jesus Christ Himself what charity is, and how we ought to practice it; for He says: "By this shall all men know that ye are My disciples, if ye love one another. Never can I, therefore, please myself in the hope that I may obtain the name of a servant of Christ, if I possess not a true and unfeigned charity within me".

No matter the size and extent of charities there is always need for the little acts of kindness of people to people. Jesus spoke of the cup of cold water. A kindness may be just a comforting presence to someone alone and lonely, the provision of a listening ear and an understanding heart. "They serve God who serve his creatures". We all have our problems but they should not be allowed to blind us to those of others or discourage us from helping them.

When a Chicago heiress was suffering from an obscure disease her parents learned of the one surgeon who was successful in this field. He was Dr. Adolf Lorenz of Vienna. He came on their plea and performed a successful operation on the girl. Engaged to give a lecture at a university in a mid-western town he went for a walk and as night fell he got caught in a thunderstorm. Soaking wet and miserable, he sought shelter in the only house in sight to be told by the lady at the door, "Go away we have trouble enough here". Lorenz tramped on until found by anxious friends. Next day the lady who had refused shelter to an unwelcome caller was shocked to learn that she had turned from her door the man she had been trying to contact to treat her sick child. The moral of the story is - never refuse to help another for kindness is often of mutual benefit. Oliver Goldsmith advised, "Learn the luxury of doing good".

In the life of Jesus there are many illustrations on how people should conduct themselves. His healings were responses to human need. Paul in his great poem, First Corinthians 13, spells out what charity is and how it affects the lives of people who take seriously the obligations of personal, family and society duties and responsibilities. To accept what Paul writes is to conclude that "there is no Christianity where there is no charity".

Charity is never restricted to giving money or goods, there is constant and clamant need of it in thinking and speaking in a society like ours where we have suffered continuously and grievously from wrong thinking and the terror of the tongue.

Pride: the first of sins

In its beginning days Christians listed sins to be regarded as more detestable than others - the Seven Cardinal Sins: pride, coveteousness, lust, anger, gluttony, envy and sloth. The order changed at times but pride always came first. It is the sin constantly condemned in the Scriptures. The Psalmist says: "Even though the Lord is so high above He cares for the lowly, and the proud cannot hide from Him: (138:6). Proverbs repeats that, "Six things the Lord hates, seven things are detestable to Him: a proud eye, a false tongue, hands that shed innocent blood, a heart that forges thoughts of mischief, and feet that run swiftly to do evil, a false witness telling a pack of lies, and one who stirs up quarrels between brothers": (6:16-19) and "Proud men, one and all, are abominable to the Lord; depend upon it; they will not escape punishment" (16:5). Isaiah has this, "Man's proud eyes shall be humbled, the loftiness of men brought low, and the Lord alone shall be exalted....." (2:11). Luke quotes Mary, "the arrogant of heart and mind He has put to rout" (1:51) and Paul told the Christians at Philippi, "There must be no room for rivalry among you, but you must humbly reckon others better than yourselves. Look at each other's interest and not merely to your own" (2:3,4).

Pride is a sin which persists. It is to be found in all sorts and conditions of men, and women, and Christians are never exempt from a "condition" which has the most serious consequences for them in their witness to Christ. Many of us have found it hard to "pour contempt on all my pride." It is a subtle sin even deceiving some who believe themselves to be humble of heart. There is the contradiction. It is possible to be proud of one's humility. A preacher on pride was told by a parishioner, "Humility is my forte."

Pride has many appearances, physical, intellectual; of family, class, property. It is boastful and critical. Speaking well of self, it states or suggests inferiority in others. Jesus highlighted the sin of pride in the story of the Pharisee and the tax-collector when they prayed in the temple. The one came to pray about himself and the other to ask God for forgiveness for himself. It ends, "For everyone who exalts himself will be humbled, and he who humbles himself will be exalted" (Luke 18:9-14).

Pride in the Christian is a refusal to copy Christ in the pattern for living He set in the days of His flesh. Some find it difficult to take the lesser place, though many of the early Christians who were most effective for Christ were willing to play supporting roles. Among them were Andrew, Philip and Barnabas.

Humility shows in ordinary and extraordinary situations and circumstances. In how we value other people, how we react to them and accept or reject them. Lack of humility shows when we are so adamant that we are in the right that we will not take heed of another's opinion even in complex matters when contrary opinions are to be expected and welcomed . Proverbs has this warning, "A fool thinks he is always right; wise is the man who listens to advice" (12:15).

The test of the wise man in the Scriptures is that he is humble, willing to be advised, criticised and corrected. The refusal to recognise this has destroyed fellowship among Christians and split churches.

Pride has always divided Christians. It caused the disciples to argue about who should be the leaders among them (and that while travelling with Jesus towards Calvary). It happened in the church at Philippi for Paul pleaded, "Euodia and Syntyche, please, I beg you, try to agree as sisters in the Lord" (4:2). It was the attitude Paul condemned when some claimed special relationships as proud boasts of their standing among the others.

The antidote for pride is to have a proper relationship with Christ to determine to copy Him in how He thinks and acts, to be humble as He was humble. How He humbled Himself is spelled out in Philippians 2:6-11: "Who, being in very nature God, did not consider equality with God something to be grasped, but made Himself nothing taking the very nature of a servant, being made in human likeness. And being found in appearance as a man, He humbled Himself and became obedient to death - even death on a cross. Therefore God exalted Him to the highest place and gave Him the name that at the name of Jesus every knee should bow, in Heaven and on earth and under the earth, and every tongue confess that Jesus Christ is Lord to the glory of God the Father".

Someone prayed for humility in these words: "Lord, bend that proud and stiff-necked I, help me to bow the neck and die, beholding Him on Calvary, who bowed His head for me."

Another man believed that we have not learned the first letter of the word Christian until our 'I' has been bent into a 'C'. Not I, but Christ."

The judgement of Christ

"For everyone of us will have to stand without pretence before Christ our Judge, and we shall be rewarded for what we did when we lived in our bodies whether it was good or bad." 2 Corinthians 5:10.

"Judgement: the inevitability of a reckoning." "To every soul there is a day of reckoning."

We are all and always under judgement - of God, of other people and of ourselves. A sense of coming judgement should enliven our consciences, produce sensitivity to the needs of our common humanity; a persuasion for good conduct; and an acceptance of responsibility and liability for others. We live in a world good for some, bad for many more.

The Christian is to be an example to other people in selflessness, honesty, generosity and sympathy. He should be seen as one who is anxious to live for Jesus and to think and act as He would in his personal and community relationships. But regrettably, he can be a poor example in Christian living. This happens when Christian values are discounted and lesser standards substituted.

The judgement of God

There is no hiding from Him who will call us to account for our words and deeds. His judgement will be fair, just and merciful. Jesus demonstrated that in His treatment of people - their abilities and strengths, weaknesses and inadequacies.

"For the love of God is broader than the measure of man's mind, And the heart of the Eternal is most wonderfully kind."

When we think of the judgement of God it should not be fearfully, for God is good. But we must not presume on His goodness for there is what has been called the other side of God's love, the wrath of God against sin and the sinner who refuses to repent of his sins and to seek the divine forgiveness. It is always generous, for God always desires the good of people.

It is said in John 3:16 that:

"....God loved the world so much that He gave His only Son, so that everyone who believes in Him should not be lost, but should have eternal life. You must

understand that God has not sent His son into the world to pass sentence upon it, but to save it through Him."

The objective of the Gospel is to reiterate the realities - the corruption of humanity; their redemption by the work and worth of Jesus Christ. Martin Luther said:-

"The sweetness of the Gospel lies mostly in pronouns, as me, my, thy, 'Who loved me and gave Himself for me.'"

Just as by choice people have faith in Christ so by refusal they reject him and that refusal means that condemnation is self inflicted.

The judgement of others

Our lives are governed by laws and customs of the society in which we live. We are required to meet the demands it makes upon us. Most people find that no great hardship for they are worthy citizens willing to share and work for the common good.

The Gospel lays emphasis on the duty of the Christian to be a good citizen. He is responsive to it when he does what he can to break down the barriers which divide people by class, creed, colour, sex or race.

St. Paul states the position:

"Gone is the distinction between Jew and Greek, slave and free man, male and female - you are all one in Christ Jesus." Galations 3:28.

Christians are judged on how they resemble Christ. When they impress people they are like Him in their attitude to and treatment of others.

When they repel people it is because they misrepresent Him and hurt Him.

The judgement of self

Conscience persuades us to do what is lawful and right and not to shame ourselves. The Christian is always examining himself to ensure that he lives responsive to the leading of Christ, aware of what is expected of him as a Christian. He judges himself.

His judgement of others should be charitable.

> *"The most generous and merciful upon the faults of others, are always the most free from fault themselves."* Aughey.

But when all is said the primary necessity is to recognise that we are under the judgement of God. To get right with God is our constant need, other relationships are best when based on that pivotal relationship.

The mystery of the cross

"For Christ suffered for you and left you a personal example, and wants you to follow in His steps....... And He personally bore our sins in His own body on the Cross, so that we might be dead to sin and be alive to all that is good. It was the suffering that He bore which has healed you." 1 Peter 2:24.

The Cross remains the enduring symbol of the Christian religion. It is the dominating theme in Christian art and architecture. And yet it is an unlikely symbol for people love life and the Cross points to death; they love victory but the Cross tells of defeat.

Strange then that the Cross came to be chosen as something for which to be proud and not ashamed; that it was declared to be

"the final demonstration of human sin and folly the ultimate expression of human jealousies and contrariness .... the sign of the inner tragedy of all human existence."

But while the Cross illustrates the weaknesses and ignorances of humanity in its treatment of Jesus it also speaks of self-sacrifice, courage and dependence on God. The man on the Cross showed that He was able to retain his faith untouched by the most awful suffering from human cruelty. He made the Cross, not one of defeat but of victory, not of death but life. It was:

"the outward and visible sign that the inner life of God can not be touched even by the darkest devices of sinful human nature."

The story of the Cross of Calvary and the crucifixion of Jesus has so affected people that many have found faith in Him as they realised what He did for them by the Cross. It showed the extent to which God would go to bring people to Himself in faith and love.

The fact that men see God in the face of Jesus Christ is proved in the Cross of Christ which says so much about the self-sacrifice of Christ. His supreme courage and disinterest in His personal safety, is the reminder that in everything He said and did in the days of His flesh, He was saying that God is like this. By Him the people were shown God as He is for when Jesus fed the hungry, healed the sick, comforted the bereaved. He was telling them that this is how God cares for you.

The great single truth of the Christian faith is that God is like Jesus. And the Cross means people can say, "God loves me enough to do that for me."

Peter Abelard said, "If only men could see the Cross, the awfulness of sin, and the wonder of God, they would hate sin and adore God."

The reality is that to many the Cross represents something that happened long ago which does not affect their thinking about God and themselves. There are those to whom the Cross of Jesus is an irrelevancy for they do not want to see life as He saw it. God and people as He saw them or to live by a code of conduct which demands standards of morality and decency disagreeable to them.

The Cross is so offensive to them that in all ages they have wanted to be rid of it, and to deny that it has any value to them in their secular world. The cross, though, is the reminder to them that if the human race is to triumph in the conflict between the flesh and the spirit. Good and evil, the lower and higher natures, it must see the cross and what it represents as the victory sign by which to conquer the sins of the world.

The Cross was not an end but a beginning, for Christ lives on in people and by His Church whenever and wherever He is made known.

It is the task of the Christian and the church to tell people everywhere, and all the time, of the significance of the Cross and what it means to God and to people in His relationships with them.

> "At the Cross, at the Cross where I first saw the light.
> And the burden of my heart rolled away,
> It was there by faith I received my sight.
> And now I am happy all the day."

This was a simple rhymed testimony of one man's experience. Such an experience is often echoed by others in words applicable and appropriate for them.

The song for everyone

Few songs sacred or secular can claim such unqualified approval as that accorded the 23rd Psalm.

Few have the permanence which keeps it fresh and timely after thousands of years of use. It enshrines a message for every generation for it deals with the deepest thoughts and emotions of people who are concerned about their lives and their relations with God.

The Psalmist's faith and trust in God is described in memorable words with always topical connotation for what he describes as his experience of God is a sentiment to be used by all those who share his faith in God.

The Psalm is used so extensively that our indebtedness to the Psalmist is incalculable. If we are looking for divinely-inspired thinking and writing here it is. The Psalmist is markedly simple, and economical, in his use of words. Though the Psalm comes out of the mysterious East and a way of life very different from that of much of the world the fact that it is applicable to those who believe in God is to accept that whatever changes there are in the world the basic needs of people remain constant. Peace of mind and contentment of soul are always to be sought after.

The Psalmist sees God as the Good Shepherd where others thought of Him differently – as the great King resplendent in heaven, "O Lord, you are my God and King," as the great judge, "Judge eternal throne in splendour," and as the great architect of the universe, "When I consider the heavens the work of your fingers."

The Psalmist in his pastoral setting sees how the shepherd tends his sheep and supplies their every need, and God to him is the Good Shepherd who cares for him like that and so he says: "He makes me to lie down in green pastures. He leads me beside the still waters." In the East at noon when the sun is at its fullest the shepherd settles his flock in a green shaded hollow until the intense heat has passed.

He compares that with how God in the heat and burden of the day brings him to the quiet place of rest and refreshment, and keeps him in safety until the heat has abated. Because the shepherd he sees at work leads his sheep he speaks of the Good Shepherd leading him. "He restores my soul." "He restores my failing health. He helps me to do what honours Him the most."

In Hebrew "restore" is to turn back. The Psalmist says, just as the ever watchful shepherd turns back straying sheep, God keeps him on the right road, "guarding and guiding all the way."

And even should the way lead through "the valley of the shadow of death," the glen of gloom and the depth of despair, he is safe in the company and strength of the Good Shepherd of whom he says, "You are with me, your rod and your staff comfort me."

The shepherd's weapon of defence against wild beasts was his rod, a short thick club; the staff was a crook, with which to pull the sheep to safety from danger. With them he guards his sheep against attack and from the death which lurks in the dark in the shape of a wild beast or a human set to steal or kill them.

Rehbany, the Syrian writer, author of "The Syrian Christ" tells of Yussuf, a shepherd, and how he defended his sheep. Yussuf helped him to understand what the Psalmist meant when he referred to "the valley of the shadow of death." Paul echoed the Psalmist when out of his experience he said: "I know the one in whom I have placed my confidence; and I am perfectly certain that He is able to keep that which I have put into His hands".

The Psalmist changes course when he has the Good Shepherd become the Bountiful Host. "You prepare a table before me in the presence of my enemies; You anoint my head with oil, my cup runs over." The oil and the cup bespeak the thoughtfulness and generosity of the host. But what of "in the presence of my enemies."

The law of the desert decreed that the Bedouin sheik must give shelter to the fugitive who seeks his protection so that while he has the sheik's hospitality his foes will not harm him. Using that thought the Psalmist says: "Keep away all you who would do me harm. God is my host and my protector and I fear not what men may do to me."

Succour, protection and guidance are God's gifts to the Psalmist. In that certainty he rejoices, "Surely your goodness and love shall be with me as long as I live. Your house will be my home for ever."

No image has appealed more to the Christian than that of Jesus the Good Shepherd, a description He applied to Himself. For the Christian believes that his faith in Christ guarantees his safety, salvation and satisfaction; that peace and joy are found in Him.

The Psalm to the Christian is a constantly repeatable statement of what he believes about God and how he should live with people because of his faith in God "who loves each one of us as if there was but one of us to love."

The Gospel in a nutshell

"For God so loved the world, that he gave His only begotten Son, that whosoever believeth in Him should not perish, but have everlasting life," John 3:16.

H. Montgomery Hyde in his life of Lord Carson of Duncairn tells that in June 1935 he caught bronchial pneumonia. It looked as though at 80 years of age he would not survive. He died aged 81. Only a few family and friends were allowed to see him. One visitor was Dr. C.F. D'Arcy, the Church of Ireland Archbishop of Armagh, an old friend. In their brief conversation Carson told him: "I have seen much to shake my faith, and what remains with me is no more than what I learned at mother's knee – God so loved the world….." D'Arcy assured him: "If you believe that that's enough."

Many have favourite bible texts but John 3:16 has been described as "The Gospel in a Nutshell." It proves that the most important and profound truths can be presented in simple language, with an economical use of words.

When Charles A. Dana was editor of the New York Sun, he assigned an event to a young cub-reporter telling him that he would have a certain space for his report. When the young fellow protested that it was not enough, Dana told him, "Son, get a copy of the Bible and read Genesis chapter one. You'll find that the whole story of the creation of the world is told in 600 words."

No one understood better than Jesus the value of simplicity and brevity in speech. There are His incomparable stories which have not an unnecessary word. He used language the people could understand, ideas and illustrations familiar to them, and encouraged them to think about their every day situations.

Christians have to accept the fact that they would be much better witnesses for Christ if they learned to speak as He did and do as He did. Brevity may be the soul of wit, it is the heart of Christian preaching and teaching. It is essential in communication in consequential matters of whatever kind.

During the American Civil War a memorial service was held at Gettysburg cemetery with Edward Everett, president of Harvard University, and Governor of Massachusetts, senator and orator as the main speaker. The President of the United

States, Abraham Lincoln was invited to make a few remarks. He spoke for a few minutes. It was his famous Gettysburg address, which has these lofty sentiments:

> *"That we highly resolve that these dead shall not have died in vain; that this nation under God, shall have a new birth of freedom; and that government of the people by the people and for the people shall not perish from the earth."*

Few Americans could quote anything said by Everett in a lengthy speech, but many are able to repeat the inspiring words of Abe Lincoln.

John 3:16 is a prime example of the economical use of words. It tells what we need to know about God, His treatment of people, the provision He made to bring them into a personal, proper and permanent relationship with Him through Jesus Christ. The most telling expression of God's love was in the most compelling language of all, a human life. We see God in the person of Jesus Christ.

The primary information from John 3:16 is that God loves people and showed it plainly when in the man Jesus He took flesh with the single purpose of bringing people into a loving relationship with Himself. "God so loved that He gave ...."

The love of God for mankind is reciprocal. It is always "we love Him because He first loved us." Jesus showed us God as He is – the Father who cannot be happy until His wandering children come home to Him. And what He is not like – an absolute ruler who demands blind obedience from every one of his subjects.

The text tells us of the width and reach of God's love, the world and everyone in it. St. Augustine put the thought in a few words,

> *"God loves each one of us, as if there was only one of us to love." "Could we with ink the ocean fill, and were the heavens of parchment made, were every stalk on earth a quill. And every man a scribe by trade. To write the love of God above, would drain the ocean dry, nor would the scroll contain the whole, though stretched from sky to sky."*

The love of God is conditional in that there must be an individual response to it. Love of God is expressed meaningfully in worship with the people of God, the church; and in service for others who may or may not be of "the household of faith."

Selflessness in the pattern of Jesus should be a characteristic in the every day and every way of the Christian's life.

'The milk of human kindness'

"Be kind to one another ..." Ephesians 4:30. And the little girl prayed: "O Lord, make all the bad people good and all the good people kind."

Kindness is the most attractive human virtue. Other virtues are necessary where people share time and place – patience, courage, sympathy, sincerity and honesty are essentials for those who would live usefully and happily with family, friends and neighbours. They make us appreciated and respected by others. But they are lesser in value to kindness for they may have little or no genuineness about them. The kind hearted are of all classes, colours and creeds; rich and poor; young and old; saints and sinners; educated and illiterate. They feel deeply for those who need help and they respond practically and effectively and their kindness is often appreciated and sometimes reciprocated. And their kindness is often anonymous. Kindness in the home is the showing of that love and respect that binds families together in caring for and sharing with one another. And that in spite of misunderstandings and disagreements, for husbands and wives and young people do get on one another's nerves at times.

We know of that domestic violence of tongue and hand which tears families apart, injures and destroys people.

To avoid such situations people must be kind to one another, for kindness generally gets a like response. Kindness, though, is giving whatever is needed without thought of reward.

Kindness is for the home, work, play and in the community. Life is not made up with great deeds and sacrifices only but by people doing ordinary kindnesses.

> *"Since trifles make the sum of human things, and half our misery from our foibles springs; Since life's best joys consist in peace and ease, And few can save or serve, but all may please; Oh let the ungentle spirit learn from hence, A small unkindness is a great offence, Large bounties to restore we wish in vain, But all may shun the guilt of giving pain." (Hannah Moore).*

Good neighbourliness is integral to a caring community. It has been the one thing different between the modern urban and rural communities. Country people knew one another and were kind to each other. In towns and cities neighbouring is little known because people do not have, or want to have, close relationships near at hand.

However the need to secure one's privacy should never exclude kindness and care for others.

> *"That last portion of a good man's life, His little, nameless, unremembered acts of tenderness and love." (William Wordsworth).*

Kindly relations, people with people, are desirable in a good society. It is to be expected among Christians so that it is recognised to be entirely out of place and character when they are unkind to one another.

There can be no greater indictment on the Churches than that they allow their differences to separate Christians from Christians. Not separateness but togetherness was the prayer of Jesus for those who followed Him. Kindness was personified in Him and in his treatment of everyone. It is a characteristic of the Christian who takes his faith seriously.

There are these simple rules of behaviour – that we do and say nothing unkind to anyone; that we never hurt anyone by how we treat them; that if we can't say something good about someone we say nothing.

The kind are like Jesus, they lift people up. The unkind are unlike Him, they put people down.

F.W. Faber reminds us: *"For the love of God is broader than the measure of man's mind, and the heart of the eternal is most wonderfully kind."*

Judge not – don't be a judge

"Do not judge, or you will be judged. For in the same way you judge others, you will be judged …." Matthew 7:1-2.

Jesus advised people against two human frailties when He said that they should not worry themselves and they should not judge others. Don't worry: don't judge. When He urged people not to judge others He was not advocating the abandonment of the rule of law and law-courts. Society, in order to maintain itself, must demand that its citizens live within the stipulations and regulations laid down by its administration. There has to be recognised patterns of behaviour to ensure the security and well-being of its people. It is a basic requirement of citizenship in a good society that the citizen obeys the laws of the land, and lives not for himself alone but with and for others. Life should be regulated and disciplined.

Jesus was not decrying that thoughtful, careful discernment which weighs up something before it accepts or rejects it. On the contrary He always commended the studied thoughtfulness which has in it patience and prudence. He is persuading us to "gently scan our brother man." J B Phillips quotes Jesus, "Don't criticise people and you will not be criticised." The thought is not original to our Lord. The rabbis taught that "he who judges his neighbour favourably will be judged favourably by God." They laid it down that there were six great works which brought credit in this world and profit in the next – study; visiting the sick; hospitality; devotion in prayer; education of children in the Jewish law; and thinking the best of other people.

This direction to be kindly disposed to others was a constant requirement of Jesus. There are so many examples of misjudgement of people by people that they are warnings to us not to do likewise. There are good reasons why we should not stand in judgement on other people. First we may not know the facts about them and what has happened to them. Rabbi Hillel advised his students: "Do not judge a man until you have come into his circumstances and situations." To know all could be to forgive all.

> *In men whom men condemn as ill, I find so much of goodness still; In men whom men pronounce divine, I find so much of sin and blot, I do not dare to draw a line, Between the two, where God has not.*

It is almost impossible for anyone to be strictly neutral in his judgements. That is why the state tries so hard to impersonalise justice, to treat everyone equally. We are being swayed constantly by our instinctive attitudes to people. "I don't like him but don't ask me why." Goethe was honest when he said, "I can promise to be sincere but I cannot promise to be impartial." Many of our conclusions on others are not reasoned judgements at all but the result of unreasonable deductions and reactions. It is not in human nature to be completely impartial. Paul says: "Why, then, criticise your brother's actions, why try to make him look small? We shall all be judged one day, not be each other's standards or even our own, but by the standards of Christ. It is to God alone we have to answer for our actions." (Romans 14:10).

We read in Matthew 7:1-5 of how Jesus pictured a man with a beam in his eye trying to take the mote out of his neighbour's eye. It raised a laugh but it drove the message home that if we take a hard look at ourselves we will be more gentle with other people. The real importance of the message is that we need not expect mercy from God if we are not merciful to others. Jesus taught us to pray, "Forgive us our trespasses as we forgive those who trespass against us."

The clothing of the Christian: the armour of God

"You must wear the whole armour of God that you may be able to resist evil in its day of power, and that even when you have fought to a standstill you may still stand your ground. Take your stand then with Truth as your belt, Righteousness your breastplate, the Gospel of Peace firmly on your feet, Salvation as your helmet and in your hand the Sword of the Spirit, the Word of God. Above all, be sure to take Faith as your shield, for it can quench every burning missile the enemy hurls at you." Ephesians 6:11.

When Paul wrote this letter he was a prisoner in Rome. There are four "epistles of the imprisonment", Ephesians, Colossians, Philippians and Philemon. Before then he had been for 15 years deeply involved in his work as pastor, preacher and apologist, by the spoken and written word, of Christ and Christianity.

His compulsory stay in Rome had caused him to take account of his life for he had gone through the whole gamut of human experiences. He had known life's joys and sorrows, successes and failures. His thoughts were not unhappy, there was always much for which to be thankful. The church was growing and its members now were Jews and Gentiles, for the universality of the Gospel – the Word of God to everyone – was recognised everywhere. Here in Ephesians Paul points out that Christ "is not only the Saviour of the world but also the divinely appointed focal point of all activity and all knowledge. Whether it is physical, mental or spiritual. Race distinctions cannot matter therefore for those who are 'in Christ'." (JB Phillips).

In common with all other letters of Paul, Ephesians is in two parts, the doctrinal and the practical, the faith and the practice of it. It deals with the person and place of Jesus in Christian thinking, and the church in its relationship to Him. There is a reminder of what is expected from the Christian in belief and behaviour.

This passage is from the practical part of the letter and in it Christians are exhorted to put on the armour of God to face up to the enemies of God and the faith. Paul could have had in mind Isaiah's portrait of the Lord as a warrior in arms: *"For he put on righteousness as a breastplate, and a helmet of salvation on His head, and he put on the garment of vengeance for clothing, and was clad with zeal as a cloak."* Isaiah 59:17.

Bringing people to faith in God, and to recognise the plan and purpose of Christ in the world, is the commission of every Christian. Thinking of protective clothing, for such a task Paul is saying that the Christian needs defence in an alien world against those who would injure and destroy him. Among those who saw Christians in a fight against error and evil were William Booth and Wilson Carlisle, the Salvation Army and the Church Army, with their signature hymn, "Onward, Christian soldiers, marching as to war….."

In the Christian life there is contentment and conflict. An old churchman asked by an enthusiastic evangelist, "Have you found peace, my brother?" replied, "Oh yes, but I have also found war." The Christian knows the peace of God, but he is at war against the evils which hurt and destroy humanity. War and peace were joined in the life of Jesus. War when he said, *"Yet the hour is coming and has come, when you will be scattered each to his own home. You will leave me all alone." And peace when He added, "Yet I am not alone for the Father is with me."* John 16:32.

The Christian in this society is confronted with a growing secularism and materialism. And with standards of behaviour common to a philosophy of life which is irreligious, or indifferent to religion, except for occasional purposes.

In such an environment the pressure is on Christians to ensure that the Christian voice is heard speaking out for Christ, and the Christian faith, against everything that prevents people coming to faith in Christ and to the benefits of the Gospel.

Addition not subtraction:
a New Year message

Speeches, even when on very special occasions, are only very occasionally memorable. One was made so when King George VI, quoted Marie Louise Haskins in a Christmas Day broadcast:

> *I said to the man who stood at the Gate of the Year, "Give me a light that I may tread safely in the darkness."*
> *And he said unto me "Go out in to the darkness. Put your hand into the hand of God. That to you shall be better than light. And safer than a known way."*
> *So I went forth, and finding the hand of God trod gladly into the night.*

It is unnecessary to seek for a more appropriate thought with which to go in to the New Year, the past is history, the future is mystery, and here is the prayer, and the plan, to face up to what the way ahead holds for us. We are being encouraged to ask God to help us to live usefully and happily in His will and purpose for our lives. The faith in God, articulated in these words, is meaningful to those who having trust and confidence in Him, show it in their character and conduct.

As we think on what may lie ahead of us we are reminded of the necessity to shut the gate of the past and to open the door to the future. We need, of course, to take seriously the lessons of the past while listening to Shakespeare when he said: "What's done and what's past should be past grief."

Someone else advised:

> *"Let us forget the things that vexed and tried us.*
> *The worrying things that caused our souls to fret.*
> *The hopes that cherished long, were still denied us.*
> *Let us forget.*
> *Let us forget the things that pained us,*
> *The greater wrongs that rankle sometimes yet,*
> *The pride with which some lofty one disdained us.*
> *Let us forget."*

Many look back on by-gone days – the old extol their youthful times; the weak recall when they were strong; the sick when they were well; the disappointed when they had hopes. But there is no profit in dwelling on what was, the need is to accept what is, and to go on determined to live in the future as fully, hopefully and happily as we can, it could be that the best is yet to be.

Peter begins his New Testament letter by urging his readers to make their experiences in life a process in addition not subtraction. He says add to your faith goodness, knowledge, self control and the patient endurance which is the real test of your trust in God, and avoid any draining away of spiritual vitality. Your lives must not be complacent and unproductive.

The future will have its fears, cares and hopes. How we handle them is what matters. The reality, of course, is that in so many things decisions which affect us individually and collectively are taken by others. That is the reason why we live in the hope that in our uncertain political situation decisions will be taken, and things made to happen, to give us the peace, real and permanent, that we need so urgently. It has to mean that overtures, and responses to others will be agreeable, and beneficial, to the people whom they represent in whatever capacity.

We, the people, must do what we can to bring about that for which we hope. There is responsibility and opportunity to be involved in the bringing together of people estranged from one another for religious and political reasons, to change old hatreds into new happy relationships, and to prove that people can live with their differences to make a better country for everyone.

There can be no better new year resolution than the one that aims to contribute to that proper purpose. However others may view themselves and their duties as citizens the Christian, copying Christ, must show friendship, express hope and work for peace in this divided and troubled society.

Hypocrisy and honesty

"You hypocrite, first take the plank out of your own eye, and then you will see clearly to remove the speck from your brother's eye". St. Mark 7 v 5.

The English word hypocrite comes from the Greek word for actor. The hypocrite plays a part, appears other than who and what he is, says one thing and thinks another.

In common useage the hypocrite is someone whose character and conduct contradict his claim to be a good Christian. Hypocrisy is often garbed in the robe of religion. Whatever the reason for his duplicity the pretence is odious, for the hypocrite by his insincerity and dishonesty turns others away from faith. The response to him can be, "if he is a Christian, I want no part of a Christianity that has him in it."

Jesus speaks of Jews who made long prayers in public places, wore on their faces the mask of piety, went through the motions of worship but were insincere and insensitive to the importance of what they said and did. Jesus condemned such people in the strongest terms.

When Samuel had the task of choosing a king for Israel he interviewed the sons of Jesse. Among them was the especially handsome and talented Eliab, but Samuel refused him also for as the schoolboy told me, "He was all right on the outside, but not on the inside."

It was said of Sarah Bernhardt, the famous actress that while she played the most tender and romantic roles to melt the hearts of rapt audiences, and wanted everyone to see her as such a person, gracious and kind, she was a terror to work with or she was devoured with animosity against anyone she thought had not properly respected her. Like Eliab she was all right on the outside but not on the inside. John Bunyan described someone as "Saint abroad devil at home."

There are always those who honour God with their lips, but their hearts are far from Him. Matthew Henry claimed; "Hypocrites do the devil's drudgery in Christ's livery." C. H. Spurgeon warned:"When you see a man with a great deal of religion displayed in his shop window, you may depend upon it he keeps a very small stock of it within." Hypocrisy will be found out. A plain looking secretary had a posy of flowers delivered to her at work every week to the surprise and envy of her colleagues. One day a much larger bouquet of roses was delivered. The girl was shocked and cried out: "But I didn't order them." She realised, when she had confessed her little trick, that she really had an admirer. The real thing exposed the hollowness of the masquerade. There was a happy ending for her and her admirer.

Regrettably, most unmaskings and disclosures of pretence have bad consequences.

There are many Biblical warnings on hypocrisy. Jesus spoke of ravening wolves in sheep's clothing. He was transparent, totally without pretence. His life was of a piece with no contradicitons. It was said of Him: "Alone among men, his practice was adequate to his precept, so that no distinction has to be drawn between what he said, and what he did, so that his teaching only expounds his life and his life only enforces his teaching."

Honesty is an imperative in our dealing with God with ourselves and with other people. When we cease to be true and faithful to God, there can be no expectation of honesty with ourselves or others. The Christian is called to follow Christ, and to live as He did, honestly, honourably, generously and courageously; to stand firm for truth whatever the consequences and to have a good conscience from doing what he had to do to the best of his ability. "Conscience is the voice of God in the soul of man." Izaak Walton pleaded. "Let us be thankful for health and competence, and above all for a quiet conscience."

It is a matter of character and conduct. Character is the product of personal exertion, not inherited, not given or received from an external source, not from wealth or talent but from experiences of life and how we react to them. It is how we have chosen the right or the wrong way to live. On conduct William Penn said: "A man like a watch, is to be valued on his manner of going." James 1:22 has it, "Be ye doers of Word and not hearers only." First Samuel 2:3 had this centuries earlier, "The Lord is a God of knowledge, and by him actions are weighed."

James 3:17 says: "The wisdom that comes from God is first utterly pure, then peace loving, gentle, approachable, full of tolerant thoughts and kindly actions, with no breath of favouritism or hint of hypocrisy."

Mean what you say!

"Whatever you say let your 'yes be a plain 'yes' and your 'no' a plain 'no'."
Matthew 5:37

Few virtues are more impressive than honesty. Few qualities are more to be admired than the honesty of purpose, of word and deed, which determines to stand by one's promises and to meet one's obligations.

The Christian has in Christ the pattern person who exemplifies this virtue, for honesty was the pervasive quality of the life of Jesus.

Nothing can be right in a person's life if he lacks honesty. Jesus acted honestly in every situation in which He found Himself, no circumstance could make Him deviate from his honest way of speech and conduct.

John Puskin described a statue in a Venice church. It was of a man with parts of the profile seen and unseen. He called it "a lying monument" which testified to the character of the sculptor who carved it. What was seen was perfect but the unseen was rough and unfinished. He went on to say that the sculptor was banished from the city in 1487 as a forger.

Jesus who wanted urgently to win people for his cause was always frank and open with them. There was His encounter with "the rich young ruler" when He spelled out what His discipleship meant and the men found the conditions too hard for him.

Jesus preached against selfishness, insensitivity and hypocrisy. He taught that honesty and sincerity is to speak as we think, to do as we promise, to perform and make good that to which we have committed ourselves.

People generally condemn the obviously dishonest. We have laws to punish them. But many are not always or often dishonest, insincere, they are sometimes just not strong enough to stand for principle regardless of the response of others. Insincerity is at its worst when it takes on the face of piety. Dishonesty in religion is well known for there have been many notorious cases of deceit in the pursuit of the spoils of a religion, which can make the unscrupulous trader in people's innocence a wealthy man or woman.

Christ demands that the Christian be utterly true, entirely trustworthy. Any examination of the inner life of Jesus discloses His purity of thought and deed. He looked behind the public appearance of a person to see what he was really like.

It is a fact of life that people can sometimes do good for selfish purposes. To be good is the essential aspiration of all who would seek to follow Christ. It is a proper principle to strive to have the respect of other people. More than that we need to so live that we can respect ourselves.

It is possible, as we know, to show an appearance of honesty, sincerity and decency but we are what we are in our inmost thoughts and emotions. We know whether the approval we receive is earned or not.

Jeremy Taylor made the point:

> "He that does as well in private between God and his own soul as in public, hath given himself a testimony that his purposes are full of honesty, nobleness and integrity."

Longfellow described an honest man:

> "You know I say, just what I think, and nothing more nor less, And when I pray, my heart is in my prayer, I cannot say one thing and mean another." "If I can't pray I will not make believe." We are reminded by the writer of "Hebrews".

> "Nothing in all creation is hidden from God's sight. Everything is uncovered and laid bare before the eyes of Him to whom we must give account." 4:13.

It is important that we live honestly with our fellows, with ourselves but more important that we live right with God. The life of Jesus has these three elements.

The initial requirement of our Christian faith is reality, sincerity and honesty. F.W. Robertson explained:

> "A Christian is a man on whose clear and open brow God has set the stamp of truth; one whose very eye beams bright with honour; in whose very look and bearing you may see freedom, manliness and veracity; a brave man ...... a noble man ...... frank, generous and true ...... "

"Our religion is intensely practical. It expresses itself best in the good quality of those whose are truly Christ-like."

Jonathan Edwards in his blunt way spells it out:

"A greater absurdity cannot be thought of than a morose, hard hearted, covetous, proud, malicious Christian".

For Christ and the Church

"Be on your guard, stand firm in the faith, live like men, be strong. Let everything you do be done in love."
1 Corinthians 16:13.

We constantly admire the commitment of our brethren to their church. There is a splendid devotion to it as the repository of the faith expressed in words and actions which contribute to the acceptance by many in this society, of Christian values and principles.

Their loyalty to the church is of inestimable value to them and to it, spiritually, in the shared worship of God, and in forms and ceremonies often of proven worth over several centuries; and practically, in the maintenance of its structures to meet its obligations to Christ and people.

The church has had to accept changes in a society, increasingly secularist, irreligious and indifferent to what were previously generally accepted ethical standards of conduct. This is an age of revolution and the church more than ever must present the faith in words that are simple, clear, precise and appealing.

Time was when few people were outside the influence of the church. Time is that very many have little or no contact with the church or with church members, how to best reach people with the gospel is the task the church faces continuously, and pressingly, whatever the difficulties. The church has to be in touch with people, using any available means of communication necessary to persuade them to turn to Christ, to receive and to enjoy the benefits He brings us.

While the old and proven means of reaching people with the good news of Jesus Christ - teaching and preaching - remain very important elements in Christian communication, other ways are being used to ensure that the faith is known, understood and accurately evaluated. They include methods which were used for generations - radio, television, books, newspapers, tracts, pamphlets, play, film, pageant and exhibition - initiative has never been lacking. More concentrated use of these mediums and with the incredible machinations of the computer added, evangelism has widened its scope.

The talent and skill of the Christian can be used in numerous ways for the primary purposes of the church which are:

- to proclaim the good news of the Kingdom;
- to teach, baptize and nurture new believers;
- to respond to human need by loving service;
- to seek to transform the unjust structures of society.

The proposal of the Anglican Lambeth Conference 1998 was to add:

- to safeguard the integrity of creation and renew the life of the earth.

The faith and the practice of it is spelled out here in terms acceptable to church people whatever their denominational allegience.

And in evangelism there is always the one to one, person to person, contact. The Christian whose personal testimony to what faith in Christ has meant in his life, can at times persuade others to turn to Him too.

The stand for Christ and Christian values has been a charge on Orangeism from its beginning.

It is regrettable, unfair end unjust, that as a Christian organisation, we suffer from misjudgment and misrepresentation when those good things for which we stand are obvious to everyone.

In a statement of December 1998 the Order said:

> "Our thinking on religion, politics and social questions is governed by our Christian beliefs. Anything which is not compatible with them is to be refused and rejected,"

In a prayer:

> "We ask God for the clarity to hear His voice, the wisdom to understand what He is saying to us today and the courage to rise up and do it."

The absolute need for prayer

Don't worry about anything, but in all your prayers ask God for what you need, always asking him, with a thankful heart.

And God's peace, which is far beyond human understanding, will keep your hearts and minds safe, in Christ Jesus. Philippians 4:6,7.

Worry may well be the most common ailment from which people suffer. Everybody has problems and nearly everybody worries about them. It is claimed that women are the greater worriers because they are more sensitive, more aware of the responsibilities of life; more in touch with life's realities and tragedies. The responses of men and women to what effects them deeply are different, for women are more likely to express their emotions in what hurts them. But the feelings, apparently controlled by men can often hide as deep a grief.

The Bible has much to say about worry and the faithlessness and futility of it. The evidence of that is in the many Biblical references in the words and experiences of people who found it to be unnecessary and unprofitable. Among them is the advice of the psalmist in Psalm 37 with its often repeated "fret not;" and Jesus Himself in Matthew 6 with his exhortation, "Take no thought," "don't be anxious," "don't worry."

There is the recognition everywhere in the Scriptures that worry is rooted in dread of what might happen to oneself, one's family and friends; one's property, possessions and prospects in life. Worry is seen as not just concern for the future and what it may hold for us it is the distress of mind which comes from a lively imaginings of what it could bring us. And worries come not only about the future but, from fretting over past mistakes, and mourning over plans which went unfulfilled.

There is the worry from pride, self-consciousness and annoyance over mistakes, indiscretions and misunderstanding that have not been possible to redress. To keep them in mind, except to determine not to repeat them, is a waste of thought and a barrier to mental progress.

Because self-interest is the cause of many of our worries we need to keep reminding ourselves that our lives are for sharing with others. We are living really when how we live is affected by our relationships with them. Christians are encouraged to see life in these relationships with other people and in our dependence on God for the quality and values of our lives to him and to them. We are to be disciplined and controlled by our commitment to Jesus Christ and by our trust in him for the everyday things of life. We are required to "Trust in the Lord with all thine heart; and lean not unto thine own understanding." (Proverbs 3:5). The Psalmist tells us "Leave your troubles with the Lord, and he will support you. (55:21). Elsewhere there is that refrain, "Take your troubles to the Lord and leave them there." (cp Ps 37 and 1 Peter 5:7). Joseph Scriven the Banbridge born hymnist put this thought into singable words in his much used:

> *"What a friend we have in Jesus.*
> *All our sins and griefs to bear.*
> *What a privilege to carry*
> *Every thing to God in prayer.*
> *O what peace we often forfeit,*
> *O what needless pain we bear,*
> *All because we do not carry*
> *Every thing to God in prayer."*

Charles F. Deems echoed that sentiment:

> *The world is wide*
> *In time and tide.*
> *And God is quick;*
> *Then do not hurry.*
> *That man is blest,*
> *Who does his best,*
> *And leaves the rest;*
> *Then do not worry.*

The 'rules' for christian living are here in Philippians 4:6,7.

First: "Don't worry" because it is unnecessary, and ineffective in producing desired results or avoiding experiences which should be faced with a clear mind.

Second: "Be thankful" for everything that brings us benefits or just a simple satisfaction with how we are and with the opportunities for living happily and usefully where we are. When we grumble and grouse at people and things an old Irish saying to the able bodied reminds us of how well off we are, "Get down on your knees and thank God you are on your feet." Christianity is the religion of joy and gladness in a world often debased by sorrow and sadness. It recognises the realities of life with the good news that in spite of everything we can overcome even the most adverse circumstances by our trust in God and with the conviction that "all things work together for good to them that love God.." (Romans 8:28)

"Be thankful" - count your blessings.

Third: "Pray about everything." There is this advice, "If a thing is big enough to concern you; it is not too small for Him, because He has set you in his heart."

"Don't worry" the cure for that condition of unease and uncertainty is "to do your best and leave the rest to God." The Psalmist said, "Trust in the Lord, and do good, so you will dwell in the land and enjoy security. Take delight in the Lord, and He will give you the desires of your heart. Commit your way to the Lord; trust in him, and He will act." (Psalm 37:3-5 RSV)

Praying, listening, singing

What is said and done in our church services, automatically and repetitively invite the question, "Why do we do this and that in the worship of the church?"

We pray! We ask for a definition of prayer and the poet gives us:

> *"Prayer is the soul's sincere desire,*
> *Uttered or unexpressed,*
> *The motion of a hidden fire,*
> *That trembles in the breast".*
> Montgomery

It is the voice of faith; the expression of our devotion and commitment to God in words that convey our feelings for Him to whom we are indebted for life and who is with us in all the experiences of our lives.

Our faith in God is the governing factor in what we think about life and those who share it with us intimately and collectively and in whatever relationship and capacity. And God has given us an example of the qualities of life He wants in us. The pattern person is Jesus the Christ who is the presence of God showing us what God is like, what he requires of us and what He gives to us in response to faith in Him.

By His life, death and resurrection Jesus brings us by faith in Him to a relationship with God of inestimable value and benefit to us.

Because in our human weaknesses we fall short of the standards God has set for us we repent our sins and ask Him to forgive us and to help us to do much better. We pray for the people and things that have an intimate relationship with us and others who are our concern for reasons and purposes common to people everywhere.

In our prayers there are petitions for church, community and country where there are problems inevitably and endlessly.

We pray because we need the resources of God to face up to our deepest needs. The troubles we have drive us to prayer and prayer drives troubles away. Prayer is not eloquence but earnestness.

We listen! We know that "we should take heed how we hear." The scriptures are read and if we are good listeners God speaks to us by His Word. Someone explains, "The Bible is God's ordinary means of communication with people."

The reading of scriptures in church is never to be taken lightly. Readers need the voice to be heard clearly, the articulation to have the necessary emphases and prior preparation so that what is read is meaningful to the listener.

Listening in church is not easy. Thought, concentration and imagination is required if what we are hearing is to be of value to us. The sermon is meant to be a commentary, exposition and elucidation of a scriptural theme, a ministry of the Word. It has the aim of presenting the truths of the gospel in words and thoughts relevant and applicable to the time and place of the preachment.

The gospel is timeless while the presentation of it by the preacher is as different as he differs from others in personality and ability.

The task of the preacher is to preach Christ, to make plain humanity's indebtedness to Him and to live their lives as believers in God who love their neighbours as themselves. He speaks the truth in love, confidently, for preaching is the presentation of truth through personality.

We sing! The deepest human emotions are often expressed in song, hence the psalms, canticles and hymns which are integral to the worship of the church. By them faith in God is voiced, the faith extolled and Christian experiences described meaningfully and akin to our own with their emphases on the Christian's aspirations, hopes and commitments. An enthusiast for singing stated the obvious when he said:

"A song will outlive all sermons in the memory."

There is always the thought:

"We must not praise God in our singing in church and disobey Him in His requirements of us. He asks for works as well as words, not just songs but service in His name and for people who need what we can give them and do for them."

The worship of the church is the opportunity to give to God adoration and devotion for what Christ has done for us by the Cross, to ask for strength to meet the demands of life and to pray for others in their needs spiritual and material, for the faith speaks to everything that matters to people individually and collectively. The public worship of God in the fellowship of the church is of the essence of our Christianity.

Love is of God: God is Love

"And now abideth faith, hope, love, these three; but the greatest of these is love." 1 Corinthians 13:13.

This verse from St Paul is often used to emphasise the all pervading virtue. The most desirable attribute in Christian philosophy, love.

There is the suggestion that Paul might have added "but greater than these is LOVE" with an emphasis on two kinds of love - human and divine - the love of people for people and the all embracing love of God. The thought has the merit of comparison between the love that is the most desirable asset in human relations, and LOVE, God's intimate relationship with people.

There is no doubt that Paul in this hymn of love, 1 Corinthians 13, thought of love in both dimensions. He thinks of his own life and its progression through the stages of learning and growth.

"When I was a child I spake ..... understood as a child, but when I became a man I put away childish things."

There is time and distance between childhood and manhood, a progress in learning, thinking and doing, a continuous learning process that is endless in life. Paul is at his most practical when he describes the qualities of love. It is patient and kind: not jealous, conceited or proud: not bad mannered, selfish or irritable: holds no grudges, condemns evil, extols truth. The virtues are listed to remind his readers of the necessity of living lives that are honest and honourable, above all loving and selfless. Not just a "good life" which can be negative and unfeeling in its treatment of others, but goodness that is Christ-like in its humanity, decency and sensitivity. A little girl prayed perceptively:

"O God, make all the bad people good and the good people kind."

Paul had Jesus in mind when he wrote for in His life He clearly illustrates the supremacy of love. And so Paul describes love as the one priceless possession. Leslie Weatherhead echoed Paul when he said: *"I know that God is love ..... by contemplating the man Christ Jesus."*

Paul lists what were regarded as of importance and value and says that while they will pass away love will remain. He is joined by other New Testament writers who make the same assertion - to them, too, love is the all important. John says: "*If we love one another, God dwelleth in us and His love is perfected in us.*"

Peter concurs "*above all things have fervent love among yourselves, for love will cover a multitude of sins.*"

Someone adds: "*Love opens the book of life and unlocks the secrets of the kingdom of God.*"

Paul states a principle for those who value life as a process in living and learning, and who accept that there are questions to be left unanswered. He says, "*Now we see through a glass, darkly, but then face to face. Now I know in part; but then shall I know even as also I am known.*"

Faith is necessary! It is by faith that we are assured of the reality of God's love. But there is a time when we shall see Him as He is, and then, "*faith will vanish into sight; the clouded glass will be removed to make way for the perfect vision of the King in his beauty.*"

Hope is necessary! Without it we lose heart. Always there has to be the expectation, anticipation, for that is what makes life a journey into the unknown with satisfaction and completion at its end.

Paul's insistence on love retains an everlasting relevance for love is the one emotion most needed in this and every age. Christian love, Christ inspired and Christ-like in its performance, is the greatest and most obvious need in our society. Where it is at work the benefit is to be seen in lives lived by the help of God and in caring for others. Faith is the stem, hope is the leaf and love the blossom. They are required in the growth of the tree of life. But greater than these is the LOVE of God. Love which has its potency in the life, death and resurrection of Christ.

"*God was in Christ personally reconciling the world unto himself.*"

A prayer: "*May we live by faith, walk in hope and be renewed in love until the world reflects your glory and you are all in all. Even so, come Lord Jesus.*" Amen.

Seek the gift of peace

Peace is not just the absence of violence in the pursuit of political objectives. It is that state of mind which refuses to accept that force of arms can be justified in our circumstances. The pursuit of peace is not only for those whose task it is to secure the safety of the citizen. It is the duty of every citizen in a good society to seek peace in himself and to live at peace with his fellows. We are living as we should if we are at peace within ourselves and with other people. That is the pattern for living which when spread would change the situation here and better the circumstances of everyone. We should be the spreaders of peace for peace is not to be found in retreating from life, cocooning ourselves from people and things which would disturb and distress us.

To the Christian peace is the gift of God to all who trust in Him and God never encourages us to avoid the responsibilities and problems of life. He helps us to face them and to live with their consequences.

When Jesus offered people His peace He was at the storm centre of a world seething with unrest, terrorised and tormented by powerful malignant forces. At that time and in that place He gave to people the good news of a loving God and showed them how to live at peace with God and with their neighbours. His behaviour was an example to them in the days when He suffered at the hands of those determined to destroy Him. On the cross He refused the myrrh which would have soothed His senses and clouded His mind against the pain He suffered. His faith in God and the peace of mind it brought Him was all He needed in that final hour.

He showed by His life that when there is trust in God, and hearts and minds are attuned to Him, we are at peace. He said that harmony between God and people made peace possible. St. Augustine echoed that thought when he prayed, "Thou, O God, hast made us for thyself, and our hearts are restless until they rest in thee."

The peace of God sets the divine and true valuation on life. It put Jesus beyond the reach of many of the things that trouble us. He had no dependence on money, possessions or property. He was unaffected by the scorn of men. He knew that popularity was a fleeting thing for He had days when the people flocked to see and hear Him and the others when all forsook Him and fled. The deeper we sink our roots into the earth the more we are affected by the tremors of the earth. The more dependent we are on material things the more we expose ourselves to anxieties and disappointments.

A main strength of the church in its early days was its lack of power, position and possessions. How very different has been the state of the church down the centuries. When it became wealthy, powerful and with incredibly valuable possessions, it was often least effective in what should have been its priorities, evangelism and social work. We have the position even now that when the church is poorest materially, it is strongest spiritually. We do not need to labour that point, the evidence is in the weaknesses of the older churches and the strengths of the younger churches, especially in those countries where church growth is at stampeding speed.

Christ-like love of people for people is the way of peace. That selflessness has been the characteristic of great souls. Men like Abraham Lincoln, when people were saying things about him that nearly broke his heart, said, "With malice towards none, with charity for all, with firmness in the right, let us strive on to finish the work we are in, to bind up the nation's wounds to care for the widow and orphan, to do all that may achieve a true and lasting peace for ourselves and all mankind." There was no pettiness, no bitterness, no grudge, nothing that would hinder the coming of peace.

The lesson in this is - we cannot receive the peace of God for ourselves without wanting that peace for everybody else. "The love of God is a tide which will carry us into the lives of others and give us over to the world's agony."

Christians have the assurance of God's loving care for us. Paul describes his experiences in hard times to encourage other believers, "We are handicapped on all sides, but we are never frustrated; we are puzzled but never in despair. We are persecuted, but we never have to stand it alone, we may be knocked down but we are never knocked out." (2 Cor. 4:7)

The prophet Isaiah provides words for this thought: "Thou wilt keep him in perfect peace, whose mind is stayed on Thee: because he trusteth in Thee." (Isaiah 26.3)

Sing to the Lord: always give thanks

"Speak to one another with the words of psalms, hymns and sacred songs, sing hymns and psalms to the Lord with praise in your hearts. In the name of our Lord Jesus Christ, always give thanks for everything to God the Father."
Ephesians 5:20

Paul says a Christian should be living happily, contentedly, joyfully, for joyousness is a characteristic of the Christian faith. It is not always integral to the religious experience. The dominant feature in some religions is fear, dread of personal disaster if certain words and acts are not performed and set patterns of behaviour followed. The rules and regulations are so restrictive, impersonal and fearful in their consequences if not kept, that joy is not to be anticipated where duty predominates.

The Christian faith when it is true to Christ is free of the restrictive regulations laid down in other religions. Sometimes, though, these are to be found in a Christianity which has little of the free spirit of Jesus in it. Straightjacketed Christianity which is selective and exclusive when the faith of Jesus is selective and inclusive is alien to the spirit of Christ and that of Christ-centred believers in Him. We are acquainted with those who in their assemblies are self-satisfied, cocooned from others who call themselves Christians. They ask in them for an obedience so demanding and curtailing that the joys of shared faith with others, who often differ from them in incidentals rather than consequentials, are lost to them.

That picture of Christians disagreeing and attacking one another and in the name of the God whose intention is to unite them in brotherly love is a put off to people who are being shown something other than what God wants. It is the evidence of sectarian preferences which is a denial of the oneness of believers in Jesus Christ.
Practical differences among Christians are often theological and philosophical when what is most attractive, pleasing and beneficial in Christianity is its practical, purposeful and sensitive service for people, who are impressed when Christians bring their joy into their lives. The Christian who lifts the spirit of others is like the medical missionary who had such a happy face that when he made his ward rounds it was said, "Half the disease left the patients when they saw him."

Paul provides the recipe for Christian joy. He says we should be thankful for everything, for we are ever in debt to Christ and recipients of the goodness of God. Our praises should be continuous, private and public expressions of our faith. Our thanks are for all things. That includes the dark clouds of adversity as well as the sunshine of success. Job made this response in his sufferings when he said, "Let God deal with me as He will, I will welcome His dealings with thanksgiving." To think like this is to believe that all things do work together for good to them that love God. We may have trouble with that for we have limited vision but we must not allow our impaired sight to hinder us in our Christian living. We have the promises of God as the proof of his goodwill towards us. Jesus lived in the certainty that to have God's promises was to have what He promised.

Positive gratitude to God can be lost in grumbling about life; silenced in petulant complaints on the conduct of other people. We have to learn that "Gratitude is the soil on which joy thrives." Positive thinking is energising and constructive. Negative thinking is disabling and destructive. We need the conviction of Paul and to echo him, "I can do all things through Christ who strengthens me."

Judgement is four-fold

*"Shame on the tyrant city, filthy and foul.
No warning voice did she heed, she took no rebuke to
heart. She did not trust in the Lord or come near to her
God." Zephaniah 3:1,2.*

Zephaniah was the Old Testament messenger of God to Jerusalem just before the Babylonian captivity of the city. He warned against such a fate because the people were guilty of conduct that made that possible. It happened as he predicted. When he spoke to them he saw there was no way he could change their attitudes. What he did was to describe the causes of their distressful state. He minced no words when he condemned the city and gave four reasons for how it had brought such an invasion on itself.

The people had not listened to what God was saying to them through His prophets who had delivered God's message to them simply and unapologetically. They ignored correction, refused instruction, deliberately disobeyed the prophets who pleaded for loyalty to God and for them to live their lives in ways pleasing to Him. They did not trust in the Lord whose covenant relationship with them had made their city great. Instead they had turned to foreign powers in which to place their confidence. And they tried to use these alliances to further their ambitions by playing off one against the other. They had turned away from God, the sanctuary was neglected, worship abandoned so that when the Babylonians invaded the city they found it easy to subdue people who had lost their faith, their sense of values and their confidence, for their planning and plotting had worked against them.

The Babylonians stripped the house of God of all that was of value and carried it off to adorn the pagan palaces of Babylon and all because Judah "drew not near to her God."

The condemnation of Judah and Jerusalem was for their godlessness. When they refused to hear the voice of God conscience was stifled, when they would not take instruction truth was neglected; when they did not trust in the Lord, faith was abandoned and communion with God was broken. The things for which Judah and Jerusalem were indicted are those that are applicable to our own country in these highly secularised times, confidence is stifled, faith abandoned and the practice of religion is discontinued. Where there is no worship faith is dimmed, truth is devalued and conscience silenced and God and the Church go unmentioned.

Conscience silenced! Conscience is the safety valve of the moral and spiritual life. We can not act against conscience and not be hurt. But some have insisted in doing that and it is blunted and they do as they please. And they have to take the consequences. The Christian who lives by his faith honestly, honourably and unselfishly, knows there can be no peace of mind until there is peace within oneself and with others.

St. Paul, in his defence in court with Felix the judge, was concerned "to have always a conscience devoid of offence towards God and towards men." (Acts 24:16) He told Timothy that what he preached was very important but of equal value was his character and conduct. Paul lived as he preached. He felt the pressure of conscience when he said, "Woe is unto me if I preach not the gospel." He encouraged people to answer "answer to your own conscience."

Truth rejected! Truth is not always easy to digest but it has to be faced whatever its demands and irrespective of the consequences. There can be no success for Christian or Church when the truths of God are neglected or presented so badly that people reject them. The faith demands honesty from the Christian and the need to so live that his words are not contradicted by his deeds. Many have been won for Christ by the Christ-likeness of believers.

Faith abandoned! Many of our people have little or no regard for the Christian faith and none for the church in society. The church has the task of living and witnessing to the faith, to witness to the necessity of trust in Christ and to receive the benefits He brings to all who believe in Him so that others will be persuaded to "turn to Jesus" and to have Him as the Lord and Saviour of their souls.

Communion broken! When people do not worship God they lose contact with Him and the people of God, the church. It is the duty of Christians to bring them the plan God has for them and it works entirely to their advantage. Our indebtedness to Christ for salvation from sin and a relationship with God made real by His work of redemption for us is the essential message for people to hear and to which they respond to find that quality of life.

The Book of the Law

"And it came to pass, when the king had heard the words of the law, that he rent his clothes." 2 Kings 22:11.

This quote is from the story of the discovery of "The Book of the Law" in the reign of Josiah, King of Judah. The finder was Hilkiah, the priest, who passed it on to Shammai, the scribe, who read it to the king. It contained laws, rules and regulations, and told of a way of life unheard of by him. The effect on Josiah was such that he vowed reformation of himself and the nation - back to old ways.

The book is the Old Testament Deuteronomy, the most quoted Old Testament book in the New Testament. Jesus used it to good effect. It was from it that He gave His disciples, the Great Commandment:

"Hear, O Israel: the Lord our God is one Lord:
And thou shalt love the Lord thy God with all thine heart, and with all thy soul, and with all thy might" Deuteronomy 6:4,5.

His use of this is in Mark 12:28-31.

"And one of the scribes ..... asked him. Which is the first commandment of all?
And Jesus answered him, the first of all the commandments is, Hear O Israel, the Lord our God is one Lord:
And thou shalt love the Lord thy God with all thy heart, and with all thy soul, and with all thy mind, and with all thy strength, this is the first commandment.
And the second is like namely this, Thou shalt love thy neighbour as thyself. There is no other commandment greater than these."

In His Temptation Jesus fortified Himself by recalling and quoting from Deuteronomy.

The Book of the Law was written, probably, in the reign of the good king, Hezekiah, grandfather of Josiah, who had been largely influenced by the prophets, Isaiah, mainly. Their teaching, meaningful to him, had recognition and was meaningful in his reign. But his son and successor, Manasseb, reneged on Hezekiab's reforms when he restored idol worship. The Book hidden away in Manasseh's reign was made with Josiah to give speech to the silenced prophets. A reminder of the permanency of the written word. It persuaded the king and his people to recognise that the prophets spoke and wrote what God gave them to say, precisely and pungently.

Christians when they value Biblical revelation are made aware of their duties, responsibilities and privileges as believers in Christ. The Bible can not be overvalued in its emphases on God, Jesus Christ, the Holy Spirit and people, or doubted as to its effectiveness in Christian thinking and living. God speaks through the Bible directly to people.

Robertson Smith spoke of its value:

> "I am assured that none other than God Himself is able to speak such words to my soul." He echoed St. Paul: "All scripture is given by inspiration of God."

When King Josiah heard the words of The Book of the Law he rent his clothes. He was determined to be different and to encourage his people to think and act differently. The Bible evokes response for the one who reads and heeds it is enlightened and activated by its ever relevant advice on what is of crucial importance to everyone, relationship with God and with people.

> "The Bible stands alone in human literature in its elevated conception of manhood, in character and conduct." Henry Ward Beecher.

To C.H. Spurgeon "No one ever outgrows Scripture, the book widens and deepens with the years."

> "The Bible is God's Word to us,
> Still fresh through all the ages;
> But we must read it if we're to find,
> The wisdom in its pages."

A prayer:

Almighty God, we thank you for the gift of Your Holy Word. May it be a lantern to our feet, a light to our paths, and a strength in our lives, in the name of your Son, Jesus Christ our Lord."

Trust needs to be well-founded

"It's better to trust in the Lord than to put confidence in man."
Psalm 118:8.
"Be thou true to thyself, as thou be not false to others." Francis Bacon.

"Don't do as I do but do as I tell you" is the unuttered advice of a pleader for a cause whose attitudes and actions contradict him, and convict him for dishonesty, disloyalty and hypocrisy.

We know, or know of, men and women who are practitioners in the art of deceit. Sometimes they are people we trusted when they had given us no reason to trust them. They capture us with their sales patter, impress us with their superior knowledge and claimed experiences, described at length with a blend of name dropping of well known persons who would vouch for them. Too often such pleaders are taken on their own representation of themselves, and many are the losers from placing trust in the untrustworthy.

The negative reaction to this recognisable situation, involving trust and the lack of it could be to determine to trust no one. But life would be restricted and retarded if we lacked confidence in people to whom we may be indebted in the pursuit of knowledge, the maintenance of life's strengths; the value of friendships and familial relationships; the sharing in community to mutual advantage.

The realistic attitude is to be careful in our dealing with people, perceptive in our responses to them and to be as fair and honest with them as we want them to be with us. The Golden Rule: "Do unto others as you would have them do unto you," is the one honourable stance in human relationships.

The primary plea to humanity is to trust in God.

> *"Trust in the Lord with all thine heart; and lean not unto thine own understanding." Proverbs 3:5.*

The single and most emphatic pressure of Christianity on people is to have faith, trust, in God. The response we make to that appeal is the regulatory factor in how we live, what we think and the way we act not religiously only but in the everyway and everything of life.

The deliberate decision to trust in God is a response to what we have been taught about Him by others who have shown us in their character and conduct the effects of that faith on them.

We strengthen that trust as we find strength for our living from the Scriptures, experiential knowledge of God, the worship of the church, the sense of His presence with us always. There is the pattern for living that we have in Jesus, His person and work. Our dependence on Him is pivotal in our thinking about life and death. The hymnist has it

> "*Living He loved me. Dying He saved me. Buried He carried my sins far away. Rising He justifies freely forever. On day He's coming, O glorious day.*"

Living as we do in a secular society, and in an environment often antagonistic to religion, we are pressed to think on other things. Because the Christian knows the benefits of his faith in Christ, he has the responsibility to so live out that faith that others will be persuaded to think on Him, respond to Him as the answer to all their needs.

We are required to speak of the faith in order to persuade others to have faith in Him. We speak in words and we illustrate in actions the realities of faith for there can be times when we might say: "I must teach but I must be silent." We recognise that by word and deed the Christian witnesses to the faith that is in Him. Our words are heard, our character and conduct give credence to the words. These are the inseparables in the Christian life. Listen to St. Paul

> "*Don't worry about anything, instead pray about everything, tell God your needs and don't forget to thank Him for His answers.*" *Philippians 4:6.*

Grace and Faith

"By grace are you saved through faith; and that not of yourselves: it is the gift of God: not of works, lest any man should boast." Ephesians 2:8,9.

Paul is clear, and precise, as he describes the believers relationship with God. It is dependent not on what he does but on what God has done for him. God is the giver and people are the receivers of the benefits He gives them. Paul sets his profile of Jesus, His person and work, as he explains what is God's plan for their salvation. He insists that people need to be in a right relationship with God and that comes with commitment to Christ for it is He who brings God close to people and them to Him. William Temple, echoed this when he said: "All is of God: the only thing which we can contribute to our own salvation is the sin from which to be redeemed."

God takes the initiative in His dealings with people. John said that "we love God because he first loved us." It "was God who gave" (see John 3:16). Paul would have added: "God was in Christ personally reconciling the world unto Himself." There is the necessity of Christ for "Christianity is Christ".

The sinfulness, selfishness and lovelessness in people make it necessary for God to save them from themselves, to redeem them. Turning to God, being changed, born again, converted, are how people describe the experience which comes from the realisation that to believe and trust in God is an essential of life. It is the acknowledgement that "Man's chief end is to glorify God and to enjoy Him for ever."

Sir Humphrey Davy expressed it simply when he said: "I should prefer a firm religious faith to every other blessing." St. Augustine had said it long before in a little prayer. "Thou, O God, hast made us for thyself and we cannot rest until we rest in thee."

To recognise that is to know that while the favour of God cannot be earned it is there for those who trust in Him; when faith responds to grace and shows in the character and conduct of the believer. Paul is saying - though good works cannot make us right with God when we are right with God we shall express ourselves in behaviour pleasing to him, good for ourselves and beneficial to other people. The dictum is "Good works can not earn salvation but the saved will be known for their good works."

> *If faith produce, no works I see That faith is not a living tree, thus faith and works together grow; No separate life they e're can know; They're soul and body, hand and heart, What God hath joined, let no man part. (Hannah More.)*

When Paul speaks of God's grace it is of the unmerited love of God for us. A preacher described it, "Grace is God's giving something to someone who doesn't deserve it one little bit."

Grace and faith, to have faith in God is to give oneself over to His care, to make Him the guardian, companion, confidant, and friend. It is the act of trust by which the sinner commits himself to the Saviour. Matthew Henry makes the practical point: "None live so easily, so pleasantly, as those that live by faith." To which might be added: "A firm faith is the best theology; a good life is the best philosophy; a clear conscience the best law; honesty the best policy ....."

Another describing the Christian life, said, "We were saved by grace, are being saved by grace and we will be saved by grace."

We are never alone
when God is with us

"God is our hope and strength: a very present help in trouble." Psalm 46:1

The Psalms add to their value when they inspire hymnists, song writers and singers, to emphasise the worth and wisdom of what they say about God, and the benefits to people from their faith and trust in Him.

The 46th Psalm became the song of the Reformation to put words to the Protestant Faith. Martin Luther admitted his indebtedness to it, for he claimed that it strengthened him to take his stand against Roman Catholic Church teaching and tyranny. The strength of his strength was from God in whom he had utter dependence. He echoed the Psalmist, "The Lord of hosts is with me the God of Jacob is my refuge." "God is our hope and strength, a very present help in trouble."

Those who believe in God are comforted in the knowledge that He is with them; and with Him they can face up to any eventuality in their lives.

The Psalm was written in a time of danger, despair and doubt, for the prospects of the people were not good. It contemplated the siege of Jerusalem in 701 BC by the Assyrian conqueror, Sennacherib, with the horrors that his victory would bring in deaths, injuries and destruction of homes and livelihoods. It needed little imagination to envisage what life would be like under appalling siege circumstances. The siting of Jerusalem made the siege the more frightening, for unlike many other cities it was not on a great river or by the sea. It had only the brook of Siloam to provide water for the thirsty. Siloam in mind the Psalmist sings:

> *"There is a river, the streams whereof make glad the city of God, the holy place of the tabernacle of the Most High,"* and there was the promise, *"God is - in the midst of her and she shall not be moved".*

What was threatened never happened, for by what was seen as an act of God, Sennacherib was defeated and fled back to Assyria with a huge loss of his men. This happened in the reign of King Hexekiah, 1 Kings 18:13 to 19:36.

Psalm 46 became a recounting of how God dispelled the doubt and despair of the people. In it is the determination that faith in God brings to people hope in spite of whatever difficulties and dangers beset them. There is the confidence of the Psalmist, "God is our hope and strength, a very present help in trouble."

There was always the recognition, though, that God does not promise to save us from pain, sorrow, bereavement and death, His promise is that He will never leave us or forsake us as we live through our experiences in life. We are never alone.

Martin Luther, with his confidence in God, experiences of the church, with its heresies and injustices, found in Psalm 46 an expression of sentiments and judgements he could readily apply to his own situation.

From this decision came his great hymn with these opening words:

> *"A safe stronghold our God is still, a trusty shield and weapon. He'll help us clear from all the ill, that hath us now o'ertaken."*

It is a rousing hymn of praise and thanksgiving. Its sentiments are those of Christians whose dependence on God is illustrated in their good character and conduct; their kindly treatment of others and their attitudes in what matters in society. The quality of their commitment to Christ is to be seen in how they witness to their faith in Him by what they say and do as they represent Him in their lives. Their thinking, speaking and living.

The faithful speak in the language of Psalm 56:3 and Luther,

> *"In God we trust, of whom then can we be afraid."*

The appeal of the enthusiast

Most churches have their good and bad, reliable and unreliable, members. Those deeply committed and others whose membership is lacking in enthusiasm and low on involvement. Those to whom their church is vitally important, for in it and by it they worship God and live their lives; and others who use it for specific purposes while otherwise disregarding it, and so it has little effect on their lives.

It is easier to describe those who are not good members than those who are recognised as good members, for church people have depths of devotion and levels of commitment that vary from one to another. The variations are such that some are easily recognisable Christians while there are others whose faith is so muted that there is little difference in how they live with that of their irreligious neighbours.

The church is dependent on those whose enthusiasm guarantees its life. The enthusiast is the person God used greatly to reach people with the gospel of Jesus Christ. Enthusiasts have been many in the history of the church from the Apostles, Paul especially, and through those great figures and personalities who moved their fellows in the momentous events which gave Christianity its worldwide dimension and its influence on people and places, their politics and law; morality and decency which persists even in the lessening religious and growing secularistic Western world.

Where there was enthusiasm for Christ and Christianity there were those who responded positively to the witness of the enthusiast. It remains the case that where there is wholehearted commitment to Christ there is church growth. The appeal of the enthusiast, his certainties from knowledge and experience, may not be ignored. It is unlikely to be questioned that "every great and commanding movement in the annals of the world is the triumph of enthusiasm."

Nothing was achieved without enthusiasm. The birth of Christianity and the enthusiasm that Jesus instilled in those around Him, is the evidence of that. And Christians have always recognised that nothing is so contagious as enthusiasm or so disabling as the lack of it. It is the genius of sincerity and faith accomplishes no victories without it. It was this kind of enthusiasm that Paul showed when he wrote to the Christians at Corinth:

> *"We are handicapped on all sides but we are never frustrated; we are puzzled but never in despair. We are persecuted but never have to stand it alone: we may be knocked down but we are never knocked out." (2 Corinthians 4:9)*

While there has always been a high valuation in the church on preaching, the study of the Bible, worship and prayer it has never been doubted that the life of the Christian can be the strongest argument for bringing people to faith in Christ and to the realisation of their need for Him.

The refusal of Christ, Christian faith and morality is the determination to accept a different code of conduct, one in which faith in God is unnecessary and standards of behaviour are set to suit where there is no recognition of a spiritual dimension to life. There is a devaluing of the selflessness, simplicity, integrity and generosity of Christians. But needed more than ever in modern society is the improving effects of the Christian faith. It is the weakness of humanity that people often find it hard to appreciate, and harder to accept, what is most necessary for their well being.

Enthusiastic Christians are those who will better represent Christ to the world. They are the effective means by which the Church, the Body of Christ, will be inspired, renewed and enlarged. The example of Andrew who having met with Jesus is to be copied. "The first thing Andrew did was to find his brother Simon and tell him, 'We have found the Messiah' (that is the Christ). Then he brought Simon to Jesus."

'Who trusteth in the Lord, Happy is He' (Proverbs: 16:20)

Wisdom is ageless! These words are those of a writer of an age, environment, and way of life very different from our own and yet what he says is echoed by Christians everywhere and all the time.

The peace of mind, contentment of soul, happiness they enjoy find their expression in these words. They sum up the whole essence of the Christian religion with it concentration on the essential relationship of God with people and them with one another. Jesus said this in what was his constant advice to people, "have faith in God." The Christian has it as his attitude to life wherever he is and whatever his circumstances. But clearly it is not everyone's attitude to life.

There is an old song which advises people to leave their cares and sorrows to Mother Nature and Father Time and they will make their blue world a new world. We know there is truth in this for Nature and Time have been effective in healing wounds and restoring momentum to life after serious illness and bereavement.

Time heals when it dims memories of troubles and losses to allow us to get on with our lives. The passage of time can blunt the edge of trial, bring new interests and new relationships. But it will not pluck from the memory the deeply rooted sorrow. Time will not by itself blunt the edge of trials and bring light out of darkness.

Nature, too, can heal. Fresh air and the heat of the sun for the convalescent; the panorama of scenic beauty to lift the minds of the tired and jaded. But yet again we should not expect too much. A young girl recovering from serious illness in a sanitoriam sited in magnificent natural surroundings cried, "O how I hate those heartless hills. They seem so careless and unconcerned. I want a heart to turn to, someone who understands me."

We are faced with the question, wherein lies our pleasures and expectations of life - in possessions and riches? Many have found that wealth is not the ensurer of happiness. A very wealthy old lady talked of the struggles her husband and she had had in building up a very successful business. They had journeyed from poverty to riches. As she reminisced on the struggles of the past she added regretfully, "In those hard times we had nothing but we were very happy." Henry Ford claimed that his great wealth had brought him only sleepless nights. It appears that lottery winners often find it hard to cope with their riches because of the pressures of family and friends; the pleas of charities and the predators who hover where there are would-be victims and the smell of money.

No one questions the advantages of good health. It is a reality of life that one can be healthy and most unhappy.

T.H. Huxley, the eminent scientist, week-ending in a hotel, had a conversation with another guest who was on this way to a church service. He asked the man to miss church and to talk to him about his faith in God. Reluctantly he stayed on the understanding that the well known critic of Christianity would not make their conversation into a debate with the imbalance of the ordinariness of the man and the superior intellect of Huxley. The churchman told of his faith and his dependence on God and what that meant to him. When he finished Huxley thanked him and added ruefully, "I wish I could believe like that."

He who trusts in God is never alone. He has one to "hold his hand". Isambard Kingdom Brunel was about to launch the steamship Great Eastern when he asked George Stephenson, who had invented the steam train, the Rocket, to come stand by him. He was not asking for advice or help just his presence.

It was said that "The Lord was with Joseph and he was a prosperous man". Tyndale translated that, "God was with Joseph and he was a lucky fellow."

Paul explained that in every experience he had, "The Lord stood by me," St. Augustine put his words to that thought, "Thou, O God, hast made us for thyself and we cannot rest until we rest in thee." One man said what many others have echoed, "I never knew what it was to be a man till I found Christ." But the happy man is he who trusts in the Lord." (NEB) Pascal said, "Happiness is neither within us nor without us, it is the union of ourselves with God."

> *The Christian is happy in his prospects. He has an unbreakable bond with his Lord and Saviour for nothing can separate us from the love of God*
>
> *Thus ever on through life we find To trust, O Lord is best. Who serves thee with a quiet mind, Find in they presence rest.*
>
> *Their outward troubles may not cease, But this their joy will be - "Thou wilt keep him in perfect peace, Whose mind is stayed in thee."*
> *(Unknown)*

The worth of wealth

"The love of money is the root of all evil". - 1st. Timothy 6:10.

This often quoted and misquoted verse of Holy Scripture is always apt, for money or the lack of it is the cause of many human problems.

We live in what has always been an ill-divided society. We have the very rich and the very poor: and in between the greater number of comfortably off and those whom life is a struggle for survival.

The situation pertains even though there have been vast improvements in the living standards of many of our people. Certain things have contributed to the better situation - greatly improved educational facilities; opportunities and qualifications; good working conditions; raised housing standards and healthier environments among them. These have given people a higher valuation of their importance as citizens enjoying the benefits and accepting the responsibilities of citizenship. But the poor we have with us always.

The most pressing need in this society is to face up to poverty and the effects it has on individuals, families and communities. And these are crippling and destructful of society as a whole. It would be hard to overstate the damage caused to the poor by their poverty, and what it does to those of them who are bitter and angry and anti-social against those better off than themselves. Unemployment and its attendant poverty is recognised to be the major cause of physical and mental illness and lawlessness. The young without work are prone to get involved in activities which land them in serious trouble, and for some the ultimate horror of terrorism.

To alleviate the distress of poor people is the most pressing political problem today. The policies of the government, intended to right the imbalances of society, are to be welcomed. While poverty can be self-inflicted, many are victims of situations not of their making. How to address the harm done to victims is a social dilemma of huge dimensions and with large financial implications for the country.

Because money is never unlimited its distribution is what matters. Measures to be taken to ensure that it goes where it can do most good are needed, for there is use and abuse in the social services, hurtful to the country whose resources are always limited. A penny spent wrongly is a penny less to spend wisely.

It is a Christian duty to be a good steward of one's possessions. How to spend money has to be the concern of every Christian. There is the question how to evaluate that to which to give and the purpose in giving. Money is to be used but not selfishly. It provides the opportunity to do good to others. "The use of money is all the advantage there is in having money" said Benjamin Franklin. We read of miracles. To work a miracle could sometimes be easy. There was the man who give sixpence to another who needed it to pay off a debt which threatened to destroy him. The gift freed him of his life and the giver thereafter was to think of his "sixpenny miracle". It was John Wesley who advised: "Make all you can, save all you can, give all you can."

The use of money in and by the church is of constant concern. It's works of charity are many and varied, at home and away, for Christians are often in the forefront in the responses to cries for help. Commendation of them is always deserved. But always there is the question how to justify large expenditures on apparently less worthy objects?

Criticism is aimed at churches for lavish spending on their properties. There is a well argued case for fine churches, church halls, rectories and manses, but the impression persists of a too selfish concentration on the wants of the membership rather on the needs of the community. There is the reminder that the church is not for itself but for others. Its value is in the effect it has on those whom it is called upon to serve. Success is not in possessions. It comes with people finding Christ and enjoying the benefits of the faith through the work and witness of the people of God.

We had a text for the beginning; another now for the ending, "Keep your lives free from the love of money and be content with what you have because God has said, 'Never will I leave you. Never will I forsake you". - Hebrews 13:5 (N.I.V.)

The importance of 'The Seeking Mind'

The Christian is meant to be a disciple of Jesus, a learner from Him, with the object of using the knowledge he gains to deepen his own experiences of God and to share them with other people. There is the process of intaking to be outgoing. The receptive mind of the Christian means that he is often to hear what God is saying to him. He has an open mind! A most hurtful indictment of Christians is that they have closed minds, that they are often intolerant of those who do not think as they do. And the church is seen to act as if it was the repository of all knowledge, and truth as a denominational monopoly. This charge made against the Roman Catholic Church is applicable in kind to the other churches.

Many Christians have closed minds!

They are so set in their thinking that a new idea or new thinking on old attitudes, is refused by them. And yet the characteristic most approved by Jesus was the questioning mind.

His teaching method by parable, required those who listened to them to stretch their minds to understand and appreciate his thinking on God, life in all its complexities and privileges and responsibilities.

Those religious men who opposed him thought that all wisdom had been gathered up in their literature and law. He told them they were wrong and he astounded them with his words of condemnation, and actions which showed a magnanimity to others the like of which was alien to their thinking about God and people. While there were the few Pharisees who had their minds opened so that they recognised Jesus for who He is and the truth of what He said there were many who refused to open their minds and they remained Pharisees, "separated ones", estranged from greater knowledge and final truth.

We can be farcical in our beliefs and practices, unwilling to grow in faith. But Christianity is like running water rather than a placid pool. We must be tapping constantly into the divine resources which are always available to us. A main source of growth in faith is the Bible. Scripture reading is of the essence of Christian living and thinking. It is the ordinary means that God uses to speak to men. It is essential that we let the Bible have its effect on us. It is important that we read and study it for ourselves and listen to what it is saying directly to us.

A church historian claims that the great days of the church have been those when there were great preachers and great preaching, and people responded to their invitation to follow Christ. People are won by the preaching of the gospel! They are brought to faith more often by the influence of Christians who so live their faith that when they speak of it people are impressed and influenced by them. The Christian, and the church, has the responsibility of winning people for Christ. The commission constant and continuous, is the task of every Christian. The objective is outreach to the growing number of those who are without the faith. Christians can cocoon themselves to have little contact with other people. They can live unto themselves with little or no regard for others. This is wrong, for the Christian and church, is for others. "Ourselves alone" is the negation of what Christianity is about. Selflessness should be the motivating characteristic of the true believer.

Taking in knowledge and experience to equip oneself for Christian service is an imperative. Outgoing for the good of people who might not hear the appeal of Christ if there is no messenger to deliver it, is an essential of equal importance. "The church's best gift to mankind is redeemed personality, but redeemed personality's best gift to mankind is a better world, more fit to be a home of the family of God."

A sense of humour is indispensable for our lives

"Rejoice in the Lord alway: and again I say Rejoice."
The church, in its worship and ministry, is engaged in activities at once serious, and centred on the faith with its demands on the people of God "to do justly, and to love mercy and to walk humbly with thy God". Micah 6:8.

The emphasis is on a commitment to God which affects and governs the thoughts, words and actions of the believer. Life is to be taken seriously, for living is a serious business. The attitudes and achievement are of a people who find themselves in situations and circumstances which may give them a quality of life agreeable and enjoyable. But for very many of them their environment is such that they are denied even the basics for living beyond existing. It means that while life has its pleasures for some it has despair for others. And the task of the church, wherever it is located, is to help people to live with faith in God, and to live.

Everything is so serious that that other element in Christianity is not sufficiently stressed, the "joy in the Lord." The Scriptures throughout contend that the benefit of faith in God is in the happiness it brings to those who believe in Him and trust Him to take care of them. A happiness so meaningful, so precious, that nothing can take it away. The proof is in the undefeated spirit of believers whose faith remains strong in spite of the most horrific experiences, and persecutions, known to a suffering humanity. To many, tears are ever present, laughter and pleasure absent.

Most Christians in our western world find life agreeable and enjoyable. They are privileged to live their lives in favourable circumstances and environment. Their responsibility lies in that through their faith, and the practice of it, they will persuade others to turn to Christ and to enjoy the benefits faith brings to believers.

It is always necessary to be balanced in our Christian living, to concentrate on the serious - but not to disregard the usefulness of the frivolous, the fun of word and deed that is desirable, essential to a life fully lived. Samuel Taylor Coleridge put words to the thought when he said: *"No mind is thoroughly well organised, that is deficient in a sense of humour."*

Chambers Dictionary describes humour as: *"a mental quality which apprehends and delights in the ludicrous and mirthful."*

Christians, sometimes on strong evidence, are charged with having no sense of humour. Happily that is not true of most Christians.

He was a wise observer of people who described humour as : "*a human influence softening with mirth the rugged inequalities of existence, prompting tolerant views of life, bridging over the spaces which separate the lofty from the lowly; the great from the humble.*" E.P. Whipple.

Humour is of the head and the heart! "*Many a true word is spoken in jest.*" Good humour is not contemptuous. It is laughter free from scorn. Of all the griefs that harass the distressed, the most bitter is a scornful jest. And smiles express pleasure when laughter is inappropriate.

Those with the intention of propagating the Christian faith must speak to the wholeness of humanity; recognise the value of humour. A sense of humour is the philosophy of the undefeated.

We have to recognise that it is the riches of the mind that makes a person rich and happy.

George Asaf (George H Powell) with his song had an incredible effect on soldiers in the war as they sang:

> "*What's the use of worrying?*
> *It never was worth while*
> *So pack up your troubles in your old kit-bag*
> *And smile, smile, smile.*"

These were men serving in appalling conditions, and facing a fearsome enemy who found mental relief in together singing 'a simple little song' which had a large, and relevant philosophy. The evangelist, W.P. Nicholson, whose preaching had an amazing converting affect on many people in the 1920s in Northern Ireland, and which contributed hugely to the growth and influence of the churches, was a skilled user of the serious and frivolous had a favourite chorus:

> "*Down in the dumps I'll never go,*
> *That's where the devil keeps me low,*
> *I'll sing with all my might*
> *And keep my armour bright.*
> *But down in the dumps I'll never go.*"

There is always the serious and the frivolous and the balance that needs to be kept. The end note here is in the words of the hymnist:

"Happy are they, they that love God,
Whose hearts have Christ confessed.
Who by His cross have found their life.
And 'neath his yoke their rest."

The parable of 'The Loving Father'

This story Jesus told, (Luke 15:v11) may have been misnamed and often used as "The Parable of the Prodigal Son," a better and more accurate title is "The Parable of the Two Lost Boys," but the best and most accurate title is "The Parable of the Loving Father."

The story is of a father's love rather than a son's sin against him. The main character in the story is the father.

Under Jewish law a father could not leave his possessions and property as he liked. A Jew with two sons would be required, in law, to leave his goods two thirds to the first and one third to the second. (cp Deut 2:17) It was an accepted thing for the father before he died or wanted to retire, to divide up what he had.

There was no filial devotion or loyalty but callousness about the conduct of this younger son. He demanded from the father, "Give me NOW what would be mine when you die and let me get away from here." The father did as he was asked for a son has to learn about life and sometimes the only way to do that is in the school of experience for to live is to learn whether the lesson is heeded or ignored.

The fellow took the cash and off he went. Soon his money gone and some hard experiences behind him, he was forced to take a job forbidden to the Jew, feeding pigs - the "unclean" animal. Worse than that his hunger reduced him to eating the pigs swill. In this state he concluded that he would be better off as a slave in his father's house than to go on suffering in this strange and cruel land. And so he made for home. While he was on the way up to the house his father saw him and welcomed him fondly.

This parable, "an earthly story with a heavenly meaning" uses the characters in it to say, - the father is God; the prodigal son is the sinner estranged from God; the elder brother is the pharisees to whom Jesus addressed the story.

The first insistence of the parable is that a person is only truly himself when he is at peace with God.

The second insistence is that he can only be at peace with God when he sees himself as he is and sin as it is.

The story emphasises the son's repentance and the father's forgiveness. There is the immediate response of God to the repentance of the sinner.

There is often all the difference in the world between the forgiveness of God and that of people. It is only when they reach the heights of commitment to God that they can exemplify the forgiveness that is like God's.

US President Abraham Lincoln when asked how he would treat the rebels he had defeated in battle, replied: "I will treat them as if they had never been away."

The prayer of Jesus on the Cross was echoed by Stephen, the first Christian martyr, "Father, forgive them ....!"

Jesus is saying here that God treats every returning sinner as this father treated his wayward son with open arms and all the blessings and benefits of a father's love. And "forgiveness" is explained. It is the "restoration of a right relationship in which the parties can genuinely feel and behave with one another, as though the unhappy incident had never taken place."

The story underlines the realities that repentance is necessary and pardon follows on repentance, What of the elder brother? The parable is an attack on the pharisees who were tied to the dead letter of religious observance without sincerity, sympathy and generosity. The elder brother is an unattractive character, selfish, proud, insensitive and the reminder that "The greatest fault a man can have is to be conscious of no fault." Self-righteousness is a common sin among religious people.

Humility is the desirable Christian quality - the call of Christ to people is always to service for their fellows never to selfish ambition. And that service may be in prominent positions but far more likely it will be in the humdrum obscurity of ordinary living.

There is the reminder, too, that very much of Christian service is done by humble citizens who live out their faith in their lives of selfless devotion to God and people. Whole-hearted goodwill is the most desirable quality of the Christian.

This story of "The Loving Father" tells us of the love of the Father, God; the need of the son, people; and the renewing of the family relationship, Father and Son, God and people.

The subject in everybody's mouth

"The human tongue is physically small,
but what tremendous effects it can boast of .... "
"And of the same mouth comes praise and curses ...."
James 13:6-12

Our lives are governed by rules and regulations to do with relationships and how we live individually and collectively in society.

The Ten Commandments of the Bible have been the basis for laws meant to ensure that people lived with due respect for one another. Their basis, faith in God, has not prevented them from being used by those people and nations whose faith is in another God or they have no religious faith at all.

This study is on the Ninth Commandment:

"Thou shalt not bear false witness."

Honesty is integral to good conduct in all human relationships for while this commandment is to be taken in the setting of a law court it has the wider connotation of honesty in everything and with everybody. The Jewish courts which were held in the synagogue took very seriously the testimony of witnesses. Two or three were required before there could be a conviction on a misdemeanor. The innocent had to have the protection of the court. The truth was what mattered. For not telling the truth a witness was severely punished.

People tell lies for their own reasons, and some appear to have no purpose to other people. Because false witness is about purposeful lying there can be no doubt the intention is to adversely affect another. Honesty is ensuring that what is said is true, Shakespeare in "Othello" with the thought of an innocent man falsely accused said:

"He who steals my purse steals trash.
But he that filshes from me my good name,
Robs me of that which not nourishes him,
But makes me poor indeed."

The spoken word can not be recalled.

The proverb has it:

> "*Three things come not back - the shot arrow, the spoken word,and the lost opportunity.*"

The importance of things said, whether for good or ill, was emphasised when Jesus said that we shall be required to give an account to God of every word we speak. A lie is a sin against God and those who suffer from it and it belittles the liar.

The commandment requires a careful, thoughtful, and sensitive use of the tongue, that bit of the human anatomy which James claims needs to be tamed by God. The tongue is a two-edged sword which separates the good and the bad in human nature. It is the reminder that in people there is something of the saint and much of the sinner and that is no more evident that in the use of the tongue.

The Christian should be recognisable as one who speaks the truth, uses his tongue only for good purposes and by it to display the qualities which persuades others to come to faith in God through them.

> "*Oh that my tongue could so possess*
> *The secret of His tenderness*
> *That every word I breathed would bless.*
> *For those who mourn a word of cheer:*
> *A word of love for those who fear,*
> *And love to all men far and near.*
> *Oh that it might be said of me*
> *Surely thy speech betrayeth thee,*
> *As friend of Christ of Galilee.*

Peter and Paul in these quotations state the case for the careful tongue.

> "*He that would love life,*
> *Aye, and see good days,*
> *Let him refrain his tongue from evil.*
> *And his lips that they speak no guile,*
> *And let him turn away from evil, and do good;*
> *Let him seek peace and pursue it,*
> *For the eyes of the Lord are on the righteous.*
> *And his ears unto their supplication;*
> *But the face of the Lord is upon them that do evil ....*"
> *(1 Peter 3:10)*

Paul spells it out to the Colossians, the speech of the Christian should be gracious, kindly and sensitive always.

> *"Be wise in your behaviour toward non-Christians, and make the best possible use of your time. Speak pleasantly to them, but never sentimentally, and learn how to give a proper answer to every questioner."* *(1 Peter 3:10)*

The Emmaus awakening

"We were hoping that he was the one who was come to set Israel free." Luke 24:21.

In a few telling words spoken sorrowfully, with the shoulders shrug of and the sigh of despair, we hear of a great expectation that had turned to grief and gloom. The two men felt defeated, dejected and dismayed for their dreams had become illusions, hopes no better than fantasies. It is a picture of men broken in spirit, bereft of expectations.

They will never forget their times with Jesus. The experiences they had with Him; their amazement at his extraordinary gifts of thought, speech, action; His healings, incredible, miraculous and beneficial to people suffering from loss of sight, sense and movement; His goodness, gentleness, sensitivity and sympathy were unforgettable. No man ever spoke or acted as did this man.

Because they had felt something of the spirit of Jesus, had been captivated by His vision of God, and of people motivated by their faith in Him, they would never be as they were before Jesus came into their lives. The sight of Jesus and those thrilling days with Him would be recalled easily and frequently.

They were going home very likely to a hostile reception. Their friends and neighbours would taunt them for doing what they refused to do, follow a loser. As they walked Jesus talked with them - it was after His resurrection - and he brought light to their darkness, joy for their sorrow. At first they failed to recognise Him. Why this was so has been answered in several ways. One suggestion was that as they walked towards the sunset their eyes were dazzled by the setting sun so that they failed to see Jesus properly. Naive as the suggestion appears it is the reminder that the Christian is not walking towards the sunset but towards the sunrise; not into a night which falls but into a day which dawns; not towards despair but into hope.

In the Emmaus incident Jesus showed that the complex was made simple when He explained it. They said, "We were hoping that He was the one who was come to set Israel free." He told them that Israel's freedom and that of humanity is assured by the supreme act of God in the redemption of the world, and He was the redeemer. What had happened at Calvary meant that "God was in Christ reconciling the world unto Himself."

The incident has an illustration of the courteous Jesus. He was about to go on when they reached a stopping place but willingly He accepted their invitation to eat with them. Jesus never forces Himself on anyone. It was when He broke the bread that the two recognised Him. It was in an ordinary house, at an ordinary meal with ordinary people.

These men were not present in the Upper Room when Jesus broke the bread and poured the wine to institute the sacrament of the Holy Communion, very likely they had been there when He broke the bread and served the 5,000. The ordinariness of the incident is the reminder that Jesus meets with people as they go about their ordinary lives and not just on the occasional moments of spiritual ecstacy some experience. The sense of the presence of Jesus is often with people as they go about their everyday business. Because very much of our lives is "run-of-the-mill" we meet Jesus, if we are to meet Him, in our unexciting lives.

When the two realised that Jesus had been raised from the dead they rushed to tell the other disciples of their meeting with Him. They, too, had been visited by Him. The Christian faith is always for export. It is to be shared. There is no such thing as a solitary Christian.

It was the realisation that "Jesus is Alive" that turned frightened disciples into fearless witnesses for Him. It was the beginning fo the church of the resurrection, of the living Christ, God is real to us through Him and by Him our relationship with God is safe and secure.

A prayer:

> "Risen Lord, you who walked with your two disciples on the Emmaus Road, and stayed with them in their home, be our companion as we journey through life and stay with us in our homes to the end of our days; for your love's sake. Amen."

The importance of being patient

"I waited patiently for the Lord; and He inclined unto me, and heard my cry." Psalm 40:1.

"A man's wisdom gives him patience."
Proverbs 19:11.

It may be true that "everything comes if a man will only wait" (Beaconsfield). It is certain that waiting is so frustrating and annoying that to be told to be patient is an instruction hard to obey, whatever the circumstances and whoever the sufferer. A lady though claimed:

"Patience is a virtue, possess it if you can, seldom in a woman and never in a man."

But someone exchanged "woman" for "man" to make a different claim.

We could well conclude, of course, that women are more patient and they show it in the selfless service they give in everything they do. Wifely commonsense has calmed many a husband when impatience threatened a serious rise in his blood pressure.

Want of patience has been the cause of much human suffering. Its ill-effects are so all embracing that everyone is unhappily aware of them. They are the perpetual warnings that if patience is a virtue to be fostered, impatience must be avoided or controlled and trouble averted. Patience is the determination of mind and will to think and act thoughtfully and carefully. To many it is an approach to life personal and pertinent to how they live and what they contribute to society. "Patience is the art of hoping." We are reminded that they also serve who only stand and wait."

Many things make for frustration to explain why we act and react impatiently, noisely and sometimes aggressively at whoever and whatever is aggravating us. We may feel that the reasons for our impatience justify our angry responses.

"Letting off steam" gives us momentary satisfaction when we get the grievance "off our chest." Too often, though, those to whom we complain are not responsible for the delay, and we are left feeling sorry for them and for ourselves because of how we reacted to a problem. Impatience, like worry, is ineffective for addressing a problem, and could be hurtful to our relations with others and a belittling of ourselves. We may think this statement on worry is also applicable to patience:

"Worry is like sitting on a rocking horse. It will give you something to do, but it won't get you anywhere."

There is this good advice from St. Paul:

"Don't worry about anything, instead pray about everything tell God your needs and don't forget to thank Him for his answers." Philippians 4:6.

The need for patience is constant, for life is a matter of speeds, difficulties and obstacles. If we would live happily and peacefully we must be patient with other people and in control of ourselves. We should not demand, or expect, things to happen always in our time or on that agreed with another. What we want may be the desirable, it is not certain to be the available, and often for regrettable reasons. St. James, the ever practical says:

"The testing of your faith produces patience. But let patience have its perfect work, that you may be perfect and complete lacking nothing." 1:3,4.

We should bear our problems patiently if not joyfully.

The Christian faith, with the pattern life of Jesus, has a Biblical emphasis on the character and conduct of the Christian. And patience has its place in the Christian virtues with their love of God, and of people expressed in goodness, kindness and gentleness.

The Christian faith is at its best when it is at its most practical; when Christians are effective in what they say and do for God and people. Patience is the "ballast of the soul that will keep it from rolling and tumbling in the greater storms." Bishop Hopkins. It is a maxim of life, "To know how to wait is the great secret of success."

When you think of it there is no great achievement that is not the result of patient working and waiting.

"Let nothing, disturb thee,
Nothing affright thee,
All things are passing;
God never changeth;
Patient endurance
Attaineth to all things,
Who God possesseth,

In nothing is wanting;
Alone God sufficieth."
Longfellow.

May we pray:

"*God, grant me the serenity to accept things I cannot change, the courage to change the things I can, and wisdom to know the difference.*"

How to please God

"Then said they unto him, What shall we do, that we might work the works of God. Jesus answered and said unto them, This is the work of God that you believe on Him whom He hath sent". John 6:28.

Jesus encouraged people to realise the presence and power of God in the world. Whatever the situation or circumstance in which they met with Him He spoke of God and their relationship with Him.

His stories, sayings, quotations and advice were to persuade people to trust in God so that all they think, say and do, will be governed by their faith and reliance on Him.

To the question, "How shall we please God?" "What must I do to satisfy God?" He illustrated what he described in the way He lived in the service of God and people. He talked to them about God in their own vocabulary, and their own ideas, to enable them to see and understand what He said to them and did for them.

He spoke to people who believed in God, but to many of them their faith was unsatisfactory and ineffectual. They needed something more and better than what they had. Jesus described to them that proper way in which God and people could be together in the essential relationship between Creator and created.

He added a new metaphor to the Psalmnist's description of God as the Shepherd when He called Him Father. The thought was of a father close to his children, deeply concerned for their welfare just as the best of fathers would be to their children.

Using the metaphor He spoke of the relationship of father and children when they were disloyal and disobedient to him. He insisted that people never out-lived their need of God and their losses from their misconduct in their treatment of Him caused unnecessary problems for them.

They need the God-given, Christ-like virtues of faith, selflessness, honesty and generosity which mark them as children of God.

God as Jesus described Him is committed to people and their individual needs, aspirations, responsibilities and potentialities.

St Augustine said: "God loves each one of us as if there was only one of us to love." Jesus insisted that people needed God and God needs people by which to express himself in human terms. He instilled in His disciples faith in God that was true to God. When we compare the description Jesus gave us of God with how so often He has been presented, and misrepresented, by religious people, the difference is chasmic, wide and very wide.

He is not the God of fearful judgment, short on mercy and lacking in charity, favouring dogma and the demands of a blind acceptance of it. Because this is Christianity, as many see it, it is essential in the face of any unChrist-like misrepresentation of God, that we see him as Jesus did, the loving Father to whom we are so much indebted for all that is good in our lives.

And to remember His prayer:

> "Father of goodness and truth, the world has not known you, but I have known you and these men now know that you have sent me, I have made yourself known to them and I will continue to do so, so that the love you have had for me may be in their hearts - and that I may be there also." John 17:25,26.

We shall be very much better teachers of Christianity, far better witnesses for Christ, when we learn to deal with people as Jesus did, using His methods of treating them as they are and where they are, and with the respect He showed in the treatment of everyone.

Words and actions are so important

"........... the word that God speaks is alive and active, it cuts more cleanly than any two-edged sword; it strikes through to the place where soul and spirit meet, to the innermost intimacies of a man's being; it exposes the very thoughts and motives of a man's heart." Hebrews 4:12,13.

Words are essential for communication - information, explanation, education - person to person, and in family, community, church and country. In a world full of audio-visual marvels, words still matter.

Church! Religion for most people is very much a matter of words, spoken and sung. In Christian worship they are from specific sources - the Bible, prayer books, psalters and hymnals; preachers and singers; and in the vocal contributions and responses of the congregation.

Words make you think! Those used in the services of the church are thought provoking as they speak of God and to God, and with their concentration on the person and presence of Jesus Christ in the plan of God for the world. The words have many uses, serve several purposes, with the singular intention of bringing people to God, and to one another to mutual advantage, in selfless service together. Words to be well-used must ensure that their meaning is clear to the hearer. It must be of constant concern that the words be not just words used to express beliefs that need the content of faith in them, for them to be meaningful. To say the words is one thing, to mean them is something else. The reality is that words may stop short from meaning what they say for those who use them.

To say "I believe" is not necessarily a statement of belief. It could be a meaningless recitation of a creed, in company with others, who do believe in what they are saying. Words are used to express emotions that may not be those of the user. It is easy to say and sing words in a service and to remain detached from them. There is always the danger that familiarity will prevent people seeing through the words to what they mean.

Rudyard Kipling thought that "words are the most powerful drug used by mankind." The Christian faith, with its focus on words, is continuously emphasising its practical outworking, for words are never enough to do that. The faith must show itself in actions which prove the veracity, honesty and sincerity of the words. "Actions speak louder than words." It is a truism that what is best may not be expressed in words; how we act is what matters. Christian history reminds us that the first Christians "influenced thousands to embrace the Christian faith because they out-thought, out-lived and out-loved their neighbours". They had an unlikeness to others. Their likeness was to Christ.

Dr. Billy Graham, complaining of the imbalance, words and deeds, among Christians said: "We need fewer words and more charitable works, less palaver and more pity, less repetition of creed and more compassion."

The Christian must avoid the use of pious phrases meaningless to others, in order to make what they say meaningful through what they do for them. James said: "Religion that is pure in the sight of God the Father will show itself by such things as visiting orphans and widows in their distress and keeping oneself uncontaminated by the world." (1:27) It was he who said, "Don't, I beg you, merely hear the message: put it into practice." (1:22)

It is the case that the more people talk the less likely it is that they will do anything. I recall a committee set to organise a social evening. It had several meetings in which every detail of what was intended was discussed. After all this a vote was taken and it was decided not to have a social evening that year.

The thing that has hindered the progress of the church is not so much our talk and our creeds, but it has been our walk, our conduct, our daily living. The church is at its weakest when what it has to say is not heard, for people are not in church to hear and to listen. It is strong when it speaks to people by its actions; when it is serving people regardless of all but their need of help. The serving church is the living and growing church.

This is the reality! How the church responds to it will have meaning for its future in a world increasingly secular and irreligious.

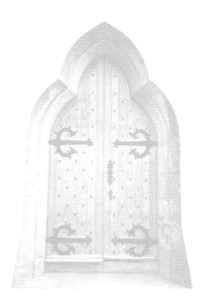

Section Two

Figures from the Bible

Micah and the Foundation Virtues

"He hath shewed thee, O man, what is good and what doeth the Lord require of thee, but to do justly, and to love mercy, and to walk humbly with thy God?" Micah 6:8.

Micah was a younger contemporary of Isaiah and the men contrasted greatly in their backgrounds - origins, training and environment. They are a reminder that God chooses and uses a variety of people for His purposes. Isaiah of a proud family was the friend and confidant to the leaders of the nation. Living in Jerusalem he was at the centre of national life with an influence on the important people around him.

Micah, a simple countryman, was a native of a very poor Judaean village. Called to be a prophet in the great city he saw it through the eyes of a God-fearing son of the soil with its multitude of people, their lives spent in the pursuit of happiness, and by means foreign to anything he had ever seen or imagined.

While Isaiah and Micah saw Jerusalem from different viewpoints they agreed on their condemnations of those whose lives were an affront to God and God-fearing people. Their message was the same about the divine judgment on those estranged from God. They differed in how to declare it. We are all children of our parents and our upbringing and the two men acted as differently as their early lives were dissimilar.

Micah's preaching brought about a reformation of religion in the reign of King Hezekiah. (Jeremiah 26:17).

Where Isaiah had preached on the constant and continuing presence of God with His faithful people, "Jehovah is in the midst of us, therefore no evil can come upon us." Micah preached on the judgment of God on people for their neglect of Him and for their social evils, idolatry and witchcraft.

He condemned in the strongest language the imbalances in society, the wealth of the landowners and the poverty of the small farmers; the mansions of the rich and the hovels of the poor.

He spoke of the judgment on a nation which allowed such gross inequalities and injustices. Those who had misused and mistreated others would suffer the consequences of their crimes. He painted a bleak picture of pending disaster when they would be conquered people, their temple destroyed and themselves scattered. Micah's prophecy was a dirge of doom. But out of humiliation, distress and desperation God would salvage a remnant who were true to Him, and they would be the real Israel committed to the well being of their fellow men. He spelled out in a few words God's demand on His people, "to do justly, to love mercy and to walk humbly...." Not justice only but justice and mercy which is the basis of true humanity.

> "Teach me to feel another's woe, To hide the fault I see;
> That mercy I to others show, That mercy show to me."

And humility - "that low, sweet root from which all heavenly virtues shoot." (Moore) Addiston advised "content yourself to live obscurely good."

Because they who know God will be humble and they who know themselves can not be proud. C. H. Spurgeon said of humility, "The higher a man is in grace, the lower he will be in his own estimation."

There is a wide gulf fixed between the self-satisfied and the humble who will always feel that their best must be improved. Henry Ward Beecher put it bluntly, "Religion means work .... work in a dirty world ..... transformation. The world is to be cleansed by somebody, and you are not called of God if you are ashamed to scour and scrub." Many of us find it hard to be humble. We resent the chores of life, the ordinary and the humdrum. But it is in humility that the Christian shows that he has the spirit of Jesus.

George Washington one day came upon some soldiers struggling to unload a truck. Standing by was a corporal grumbling at their lack of speed. Washington, in mufti, lent a hand. The job done he asked the corporal why he had not done so. "Can't you see that I'm a non-commissioned officer?" "I can," said Washington, "next time you want help send again for the commander-in-chief."

Few hear the call to be great: everyone will hear the call to be humble.

The message of Micah to the people of his day has relevance for us in ours. We stand condemned for the sins of which he charged them. We too need to live by the demand of God:

> "He has showed you, O man, what is good; and what does the Lord require
> of you but to do justice, and to love kindness, and to walk humbly with your
> God."

Doers Not Hearers Only – St. Paul

"Do all you have to do without grumbling or arguing, so that you may be God's children, blameless, sincere and wholesome, living in a warped and diseased world, and shining there like lights in a dark place. For you hold in your hands the very word of life." Phillippians 2:15, 16.

St. Paul's letter in the New Testament have many sentiments like these, prayers and hopes, that the Christians to whom he wrote will so live their lives that by their exemplary conduct they will make nonsense of the criticisms aimed at them by their non-Christian neighbours. To him Christianity is the faith to be lived, and practiced in words and deeds that prove commitment to Christ and His teaching on man's relationships with God and with one another.

He set an example in his own devotion to Christ in self-denial and a loyalty marked by such courage, patience and forbearance in trials and tribulations that would have stretched to the limit the most determined and courageous of men. His leadership in the faith meant that he had the oversight of the several churches which had been founded on his missionary travels. He watched over them with such fatherly care and concern that whatever affected them affected him. It hurt him to hear of their troubles. The early Christians had many problems. There were quarrels, indiscipline, immoral behaviour. When reports reached him he minced no words in his forthright condemnation of all unseemly conduct.

Always fair minded he was as quick to commend those of them who were true to their commitment to Christ. He had never encouraged anyone to think that the faith, and the practice of it, was undemanding. For while he spoke of it as the way to the fulness of life with its benefits and joys he always added that it involved the duties and responsibilities which come with the loyal and devoted service to God. Paul was anxious for the quality of the believers. He knew that the growth of the faith depended on the high standards in conduct of the Godly few, rather than the many, if they lacked the Christ-like patterns of behaviour. He even said that his work would be valueless if it did not produce people who showed by their lives that the spirit of Jesus was in them.

Paul had to be anxious for the good name of Christians, for they lived in hostile environments where every foolish word and dubious deed was laid to Christ's account. He entreated them to live by the example of Jesus and to realise that Christianity is to be preached, defended and proved by the Christian, who is as Jesus was to people. Christians are meant to convince people of the divine authority and power of Jesus Christ.

"The world was to believe that He had risen from the dead by witnessing and exalted lives of His followers and their moral and spiritual qualities were to be the one sufficient proof that His saving and sanctifying power abideth for ever."

The Christian religion wins its way not only by the eloquence of its preachers but by the quality of the lives it produces. There is no argument for Christianity more effective that the changed and vastly improved lives of those who turn to Christ and show the power of God in their lives.

The Christian Church is functioning properly when because of it Christ is producing copies of Himself. The Christian should always be recognisable for what he is. One day a novice accompanied St. Francis when he said he was going out to the streets to preach his morning sermon. As they walked Francis talked to people and in conversations listened to them. They had made the rounds when the novice asked the saint when he was going to preach his sermon to be told: "It is no use to walk anywhere to preach unless we preach everywhere as we walk."

We are reminded that there is no weakness in the Christian which does not cast a shadow over the face of Christ and the Christian who truly mirrors Christ in his words and actions is a persuasion on others to want what makes him what he is, his Christian faith.

St. Paul and the supremacy of real love

*"In this life we have three great lasting qualities – faith, hope and love.
But the greatest of them is love". 1 Corinthians 13: 13.*

Many regard this as one of the most quotable, inspiring and beautiful chapters in the Bible. They liken it to the 23rd Psalm and parts of the Sermon on the Mount.

Described as Paul's hymn in praise of love he uses words and thought forms to convey what he wants to say simply, precisely and pungently. It is his statement on what should be the aims, attitudes and actions of Christians, individually and collectively. He describes qualities and characteristics of a humanity true to itself when it shows love for God and for people, practically and unselfishly.

He discards what people often regard as important when he contends that only love has permanence, for love is humanity's possession of inestimable value.

St. Augustine describes it: "It is love that asks, that seeks, that knows, that finds, and that is faithful to what it finds". And Henry Ward Beecher who adds on love: "The greater lever by which to raise and save the world is the unbounded love and mercy of God". Paul says, talent, skill, health and wealth are shortlived, passing, while love is lasting.

The poem has been seen as Paul's thinking on the life of Jesus. It is his portrait of Him in His words and deeds. His dealing with people and their problems. He is telling his readers to look to Jesus and to strive to be like Him in their behaviour; their treatment of others and their valuation on themselves.

What he said here to the Christians at Corinth who often needed plain speaking and the strong words of correction for conduct that was unworthy of their Christian profession, is as relevant and necessary when addressed to Christians in very age, for the weaknesses of those to whom Paul wrote are present in all those who read him in whatever situation and location.

He speaks of those who regard speaking in tongues as of special significance, and while allowing that to be a gift of God he says it is no more to be valued than the din of heathen worship, the clanging of symbols and the noise of trumpets if love is absent.

And of the preacher whose skill in communication is evident for he works hard at his craft, but unless there is loving concern for those who whom he preaches it is of no value.

The Corinthians loved oratory, they admired fluency of speech, quick wit, the ready turn of phrase, and the ability to move people by what was said and how it was said. Paul tells them that neither eloquent speech nor speaking in tongues are comparable in value to the love that draws people to God and to each other.

There is a history of loveless oratory and it has adversely affected the Christian faith with its inflammatory rhetoric, denunciations and condemnations in the name of Jesus Christ who always spoke the truth in love, never in caustic contempt for those who differed from Him.

Someone may have a high IQ but if it is not used wisely it can be misused selfishly and disadvantageously to others. Intellectual ability can turn into intellectual snobbery to be divisive and hurtful in personal and community relationships. Intelligence and skill are most useful when made available to the community in which the able and gifted live. It is weakened when those who have much to give, give little; when what they could give is sorely needed.

Someone may have a passionate faith. It must not be cruel in its treatment of others whose beliefs are different or who are seeking sympathy and understanding in their lives.

A man was told that his heart was tired and he must rest. He was shattered when telling about his illness to his employer, a prominent churchman, he got the response, "I have an inner faith which allows me to carry on regardless of anything". Meant as a testimony to the man's faith but a faith selfish and unsympathetic, insensitive, hurtful and un-Christian. He needed to be reminded that "if you neglect your love for your neighbour, in vain you profess your love for God, by love to your neighbour, your love to God is nourished".

Someone may be generous in his giving to good causes but if he gives to be noticed and praised it is ill intentioned. Nothing can be more belittling to a person then to receive something from another who is just doing a duty and is not a giver who cares for him in his distress.

Someone may give his life but his sacrifice is in vain if its objective is not worthy of it. We know of such sacrifices and regret and deplore them.

These thoughts we have gathered from 1st Corinthians 13, but the best commentary on the hymn in praise of love is itself.

We may read, learn and inwardly digest it and live by it to our great advantage.

Privilege and responsibility: having and giving

"Listen, Israelites to these words that the Lord addresses to you, to the whole nation which he brought up from Egypt; for you alone have I cared among all the nations of the world; therefore will I punish you for all your iniquities." Amos 3.

Amos, the herdman of Tekoa, who became a skilled public speaker, set standards for public speakers in method, content and timing, for what they want to say.

Because there remains an open space for public speaking, whoever the speaker and whatever the subject, there is always relevance in considering the ways and means of those who spoke or speak, to people collectively.

While communication, people with people, is now more likely to be by the media in its several forms, there is no doubting the value of the human voice when it is used either for positive or negative purposes.

A momentary thought will recall to mind men and women whose contribution, by voice in the public place, had results good and bad for humanity.

The Bible has many illustrations of the effects of leaders and preachers upon those who heard and heeded them. Amos was one who was especially effective.

Christian history lays much stress on the preachings of some men who like the Bible preachers, continue to affect the thinking and living of people. The one to the many, the preacher to the people, continues to be the means by which many are brought to faith in Jesus Christ.

It has been asserted that the church is at its strongest and most effective, when there is a high valuation on preaching; when there is certainty of the truth in what is being preached, and the sincerity of the preacher is not in question. And at its weakest when it undervalues preaching and lacks the sense of necessity and urgency in transmitting the Gospel that motivates him.

Amos, in his background and occupation, to be gifted and recognised as a preacher, is the reminder that the Selector chooses whom He pleases, and His choices are as amazing to the chosen as to those who know them.

Amos, of Tekoa, a geographical backwater, heard the call of God to him as he tended his sheep on the hills. His response came from the burden on his soul to speak out for God against the sinfulness of his people. His was to tell them of the condemnation of God on them, and the doom to befall them if they did not repent of their sins and turn to Him. The harsh message had in it the promise of a better, proper and beneficial relationship with God on their repentance for their sins.

Amos, the perceptive preacher, was careful in his opening words not to say anything that would lose the attention of his audience. He had their attention when he condemned the attitudes and actions of Israel's neighbours and described their sinfulness. There was nodded consent that these nations were to be condemned. The reaction was different when the preacher hit his target, Israel.

The message of judgment is always relevant, for the things Amos condemned in Israel are here and in a world fearsome for the very many who suffer in countries where the richer get richer and the poor poorer. His concentration on the fundamentals of man's relationship with God and one another is needed now. It is to recognise that to God people matter, and one by one. The injustices, inhumanities and indecencies Amos condemned are prevalent everywhere in the world today.

He insisted that there must be positive, selfless, responses to the goodness of God from those who are able to respond to the allievation of human distress.

Ability to help and opportunity for doing so is there with many people who should be moved to action by the horrific pictures of suffering that are to be seen day and daily from so very many parts of the world.

To read Amos is to be reminded that privilege has responsibility, that living is caring for, and sharing with others.

Hosea: the innocent partner

"Turn back all of you by God's help; practice loyalty and justice, and wait always upon your God." Hosea 12:6.

The Old Testament prophet Hosea came to faith in God, and to a commitment to serve Him, by a route very different from that of his near contemporary, Amos.

Amos, who was deeply concerned about the problems of the society in which he lived; its imbalances - the chasm between the rich and the poor; the bad politics, ineffective religion and lack of moral values; who felt the pressures of God on him to speak out against the evils of his time and place. Hosea's concentration was on home and family and it is in his domestic crisis, and from it, that God speaks to him and to the people through him.

He had a bad marriage, for his wife Gomer had broken her vows and her unfaithfulness had driven him to near distraction. A scene which is being repeated frequently and with fearful consequences in our society day by day, with the injured party being one or other partner, and the greater likelihood is of the wife becoming the single parent.

While in many cases there is shared responsibility for marriage failure, the reasons are numerous, and well known, from the frivolous to the fearful and the incompatible, which makes living together impossible. Hosea was the innocent partner to whom no blame is attached. There are sociologists who argue that because it takes two to make a marriage it takes two to end one.

Hosea refused to seek a bill of divorcement, even though the infidelity of Gomer is unquestioned, for he determined to keep the marriage and to hold the family together. He loved his wife and he hoped by making his feelings clear to her, in spite of all that happened between them, they could make their marriage work again. Meditating on his life and his experiences in separation and then reconciliation, he thought of God's relationship with his people and from this he emphasised the treatment of God to people. Amos spoke of the God of justice: Hosea, the God of love. He likens Gomer's conduct with that of the people. He was inspired by the thought that in spite of everything they did God loved them through it all. He realised that reconciliation was there for those who recognised their estrangement from God and their need of Him.

He heard God say:

> "*I shall say unto them who were not my people, you are my people: and they shall say, you are our God.*"

There is here the New Testament conviction "we love Him because He first loved us." The forgiving God expects His people to be forgivers. It is in the Lord's Prayer, "forgive us .....as we forgive...."

The final act of forgiveness came when at the slave market, Hosea buys his wife out of the slavery to which she had sunk. What Hosea did was the reminder that the persuasion on him to do this thing was from his confidence that God's forgiveness knows no bounds.

Where Amos despairs of humanity and emphasises its worst sins and shortcomings, Hosea underlines the possibility of repentence and sought reconciliation. It is a Biblical perception that that can happen "in the nick of time". There was the thief on the cross. Gomer had to undergo the discipline the moral law required. The restoration of the marriage of Hosea and Gomer has been used to plead that a marriage can be saved if love persists.

Hosea is not a book on marriage but about the forgiveness of God who says:

> "*How can I give you up, Israel? How could I abandon you? my heart, will not let me do it! My love for you is too strong.*" *(11:8,9)*

The "gospel according to Hosea" is of a loving and forgiving God. Amos and Hosea complement one another, justice must be done and the God who is just is also loving and merciful. Together they confronted people with the necessity for a decision that includes God or excludes Him and the consequences of it. The task is that of every believer who seeks to bring others to faith in God and to the way of life pleasing to Him and of value to Him and to people.

Isaiah: the response of faith

"Then I heard the Lord saying, Whom shall I send? Who will go for me?

And I answered, Here am I; send me." Isaiah 6:8.

Isaiah determined to save and change his country. He had basic principles which he believed were his from God and he applied them to every problem he had to face. Unlike Amos and Hosea, Isaiah was born to power and privilege. His position was akin to that of a Prime Minister. But like Amos he was imbued with the sense of the sovereignty of God. He was convinced that Israel was God's chosen people and he sought to have them recognise and live by that special relationship and to honour its obligations. Described as the greatest of the evangelistic prophets his words are the product of a considerable intellect and his literary style tremendous in its sweep and resource.

Isaiah lived in troubled times in a land suffering the effects of war. He had seen the destruction of the Northern Kingdom, with its capital Samaria by their Assyrian conquerors. That was a catastrophe foretold by Amos and Hosea. And it was the Assyrians who 20 years later beseiged and took the Southern Kingdom, with its capital Jerusalem. King Hezekiab had thought that an alliance with Egypt was necessary to withstand the attacks of the Assyrians but Isaiah vigorously opposed that plan because the religion and culture of Israel would be affected hurtfully by it. He told the king and the people that their trust must be in God, for a righteous cause must not be fought with an unrighteous partner. He warned against putting dependence on armed strength and living with the horrific consequences of war.

Isaiah had the fear that the religion of Judah would be corrupted by the beliefs and practices of the Assyrians and the Egyptians. He believed it necessary to ensure the security and safety of the faith by the separation of church and state. His expectation was on those loyal believers whom he saw as the Remnat and who would stand firm for God in every circumstance, that they would save Israel from the horrors that threatened it.

Isaiah saw God acting for the nation in the person of the Messiah, a great leader whom he described as coming not as a king powerful and magnificent but as the suffering servant. He pictured Him in his most accurate profile of Jesus, Isaiah 53.

The prophet denounced his people for their betrayal of the 'faith'. He declared, in the strongest terms, that the survival of the state was nothing if the faith was lost.

Their priorities had to be right. Isaiah spoke but the people did not listen and they suffered the consequences of their turn away from God. Down the centuries Isaiah's advice to people has been ignored.

Among the many lessons to be learned from him is his insistence that the church must never consent to what is not agreeable to God and His word.

It must be free to raise its voice on anything that affects people and to speak out fearlessly to them about anything that could be to their disadvantage, individually and collectively. The church of Isaiah before Christ was then, as the Christian Church is now, the people of God. The difference now is that in Christ the plan of God for humankind has been revealed and His place and purpose in it clearly identified.

This is weak and ineffective when it fails to address the multiplicity of problems which affect people. It is only effective when it deals with them sensitively, compassionately and honestly. It stands condemned when there is a contradiction in what it says and does.

Isaiah cared deeply about people. He spoke and acted for people. What he had to say about living in and for the faith is always relevant. Christians stand condemned when they act contrary to the admonishments of Christ to love God and to express that love in love for others; when they lack social and community consciousness and ignore the responsibilities of citizenship. The social consciousness of Amos and Hosea is present in Isaiah.

The Christian should be the most public spirited person in society. He lives, with the strong pressures of Christ on him, to be good and to do good. The Christian is the one who cares and shares.

Micah: a friend of the poor

"He hath shewed thee, O man, what is good and what doth the Lord require of thee, but to do justly, and to love mercy, and to walk humbly with thy God." Micah 6:8.

While Micah was declaiming against the corrupt politicians, and mean and cruel employers in Jerusalem, the small farmers living in Judaea and the Philistine plain had Micah as their champion against rapacious, unscrupulous landlords. Thirty years before Micah, Amos had been deeply concerned about social justice, and the imbalances in the living conditions of the people for whom he acted, as the unelected spokesman, with his plea for fair treatment for everybody. Micah felt the same pressures on him as a man of God with a conscience, and had a like determination to change what needed to be changed in the making of a much better society.

Micah is the voice of all those who in every age, cry aloud for justice for all. He was only too well aware of the abject poverty of so many and found it a most distressing task to describe their suffering from hunger and disease and the effects of having to live under intolerable handicaps.

He was very angry at the way so many were ill-treated in a society in which their rulers, employers and landlords wallowed in luxury.

He said: "Shame on those who lie in bed planning evil and wicked deeds and rise at daybreak to do them, knowing that they have the power. They covet land and take it by force, if they want a house they seize it; they rob a man of his home and steal every man's inheritance." (2:1,2)

The prophet hopes that judgment will come upon a social system, imbalanced to the extreme, and that those responsible for it will be made to pay for their crimes.

Like other social reformers Micah was a lone voice much of the time. Devout churchman that he was, he found his co-religionists unresponsive to his appeal to them to join him in the fight for a better country.

The oppressors of the poor were often those who provided the money needed to pay for the church's necessities. Their misdeeds were known, but no action was taken against them to call them to account; for conscience can be deadened under such circumstances. Vested interest and financial gain has been known to adversely affect the Christian Church.

It is the task of the church to be like the prophets, Amos, Hosea, Isaiah and Micah, and to lead the people in their struggle to make a good society, fair and just in its dealings with all its citizens. The church should be the voice of the common people in their fight for justice and proper treatment, speaking out against whatever prevents them from making the most of themselves. The church has displayed the weaknesses of humanity when at times its attitudes have been a betrayal of the faith, and the Christ who valued people equally and saw them as equally precious in the sight of God.

Micah was not a prophet of doom. He was a realist who hoped that people could be persuaded to turn to God and to enjoy Him forever. He gave us the great Old Testament statement on what is the nature of true religion.

"He has told you, O man, what he wants, and this is all it is: to be fair and just and merciful, and to walk humbly with your God."

The incredible growth of the church in Africa, Asia, Central and South America is the evidence of a life-changing faith in God allied to a developing social consciouness. It comes from a wholehearted commitment to Christ: in the fellowship of the church which is effective in its ministry of word and deed; and in the happiness of shared fellowship and concern for the well being of one another. The spiritual emphasis is effective in practical outworking when faith and works go together and we have the evidence of the church in action as it should be.

Among the reasons for the weaknesses of the church in the West is the lack of enthusiasm for the communication of the faith; a loyalty which is weakened by conflicting interests; an insensitiveness to the problems of fellow members and others.

Where the church is strong in its advocacy of the Gospel, anxious to win people for Christ, there is life and growth here as elsewhere.

The weaknesses of Christianity are the weaknesses of Christians who refuse to take seriously what commitment to Christ and the church entails in how we live and act as the people of God in this place.

Section Three

Seasonal and Topical Matters

Easter and the Essential Gospel

"As they entered the tomb, they saw a young man dressed in a white robe sitting on the right side, and they were alarmed. 'Don't be alarmed,' he said, 'You are looking for Jesus the Nazarene who was crucified. He has risen, He is not here. See the place where they laid Him'." Mark 16: 5,6.

The resurrection of Jesus was the pivotal theme of the early Christians. It was the core and climax of every sermon the apostles preached. The Gospel of Jesus Christ is the good news of His resurrection. It is the substance of the Christian message and of the Christian's faith. Emil Brunner described it thus, "The message of Easter is **THE** Christian message, and the Christian Church is the Church of the Resurrection."

The reality is that had Christ not been raised from the dead the apostles would have had nothing worth preaching and the religion of Jesus would not have survived. It was the resurrection which gave meaning to the Incarnation and the Atonement, of Bethlehem and the birth and Calvary and the death of Jesus.

The resurrection was seen as the completion of the plan of God which began with the birth of Jesus, through his amazing life and horrific death to the resurrection the final proof of his divinity. St. Paul explained the life work and worth of Jesus. he says "that Christ died for our sins according to the Scriptures; and that he was buried, and that he was raised again on the third day according to the Scriptures; and that he was seen." 1 Cor. 15:4.

The New Testament is based in the belief that Jesus Christ rose from the dead. The writers were utterly convinced of that and that He is alive for ever. This conviction brought the church into being. It keeps the church in existence. The church did not create the resurrection: the resurrection brought the church to birth. The church continuing is the most convincing evidence of the resurrection. By it defeat had been turned into victory: courage replaced cowardice; the terrified became triumphant for their faith in Christ had been fully justified. The credentials of the living Christ are the living Church.

The message of Easter is of the victory of life over death, good over evil, God over the devil. He who overcame death has opened the kingdom of heaven to all believers. The grave has been robbed of its terrors. The claims of Christ have been justified when he said, the creative power of God is available to meet man's weaknesses, and to refashion his life. This is our Gospel, writes, J.S. Steward in his book "A Faith to Proclaim".

"For this is what Christianity essentially is - a religion of resurrection. This is what every worshipping congregation is intended in the purpose of God to be - a community of the resurrection. This is the basic character of every act of public worship - a proclamation of the resurrection. And this is what the Gospel offers to our dark and ruined chaos of a world, where men peering into the future are daunted by the well-nigh impossible task of creating order out of confusion and life out of death; the power of the resurrection."

Easter for the Christian is not about a pious hope. It is speaking of his expectations and joys.

Paul wrote: "Christ has forgiven you all your sins. He has utterly wiped out the damning evidence of broken laws and commandments which always hung over our heads, and has completely annulled it by nailing it over His own head on the Cross. And then, having drawn the sting of all the powers ranged against us. He exposed them, shattered, empty and defeated, in his final and glorious triumphant act," Collossians 2: 13-15.

Thoughts of Easter and resurrection are the reminder that the great mysteries of God and his plan for mankind are not to be doubted because our finite minds can not grasp their meanings. There has to be the leap of faith, the acceptance that we now see through a glass darkly. We accept by faith the fact, "Jesus Christ has abolished death and brought life and immortality to light through the Gospel." 2 Timothy 1:10.

The risen Christ gave His disciples a commission, "Go and make Christians of all nations," a task "You shall be My witnesses," a message by which they were by word and example to persuade people of the value and benefits of the Christian faith and to point them to Christ the one who can satisfy their needs, and a promise, "Lo, I am with you always." What He requires from His disciples He enables them to perform.

The evidences for the Resurrection are the Church, the Lord's Day, the New Testament; and the Holy Communion.

"He is not here. He is risen."

Think of these things –
Ring, joyous bells of Easter

"He is not here He is risen, just as He said, Come and see the place where He lay." Matthew 28:6

The concentration of Christians at Easter is on the resurrection of Jesus with the joyous cry, "He is risen, Christ is risen indeed." And what Thomas Arnold described as "the best attested fact of human history" and EP Goodman said: "The resurrection of Jesus Christ is a certainty, if any fact, not merely of Christianity, but of history, stands on an impregnable foundation, this does, is proclaimed again as a truth of inestimable value to people everywhere and all the time."

The crucifixion had taken place on Good Friday and the body of Jesus placed in the tomb of Joseph of Arimathea. It was well guarded by Roman soldiers to ensure that the friends of Jesus would not steal the body away. On Sunday morning early when the women came to anoint the body - they had been prevented from doing that with the intervention of the Sabbath - they found the stone which sealed the entrance had rolled away and were told by an "angelic messenger" that Jesus had risen from the dead. What He had promised had happened. There were to be many witnesses to it for Jesus appeared afterwards to those who were mourning his death. The evidence for the resurrection of Jesus is such that for two millennium people everywhere had been satisfied as to its veracity.

They were impressed by the sincerity, honesty and accuracy of the accounts, became believers in Christ and convinced of the truth He taught, and of the pivotal place that is His in the plan and purpose of God for the salvation of people. The witnesses were unexpentant, incredulous and their honesty was undoubted even by the sceptical of the time.

The Resurrection was the fulfilment of prophecy; a vindication of the promises of Jesus, and proof of His divinity. The resurrection became, and remains, of primary importance in the teaching and preaching of Christians. Paul described his position as a Christian leader when he said:

"I passed on to you first of all the message I had myself received - that Christ died for our sins as the Scriptures said He would; that He was buried and that He rose again as the Scriptures foretold." 1 Corinthians 15:3.

The resurrection gives credence to the Cross for it proved the truth of the claims Jesus had made about Himself. It was the certification of God's acceptance of His atoning sacrifice as sufficient for the sins of the world. Paul explained. "He was delivered up for our sins and raised to bring us into a right relationship with God". Romans 4:25.

The resurrection of Jesus is the promise, the earnest, of our own resurrection if we have the essential relationship with Him as Lord and Saviour.

A proof of the Resurrection is the existence of the church. Nothing short of Resurrection could have changed despairing men and women into people "radiant with joy and flaming with courage". These were the very people who on Good Friday ran off to leave him to His fate and who hid themselves until resurrection day. Defeat had been turned into victory: the end had become a beginning. Without the Resurrection there would have been no church, no place for Christian teaching and witnessing.

The Resurrection means that Christ is not just an historical personage of incredible fame and achievement but an ever-living presence: not just someone to hear about but the one to travel with in the journey of life. The Christian is the person who knows Jesus rather than the one who knows about Him. Paul described himself as a "man in Christ" for his commitment meant that Christ lived through him. He said, "I live yet not I but Christ lives in me."

On Easter Day the Christian faces the world with a truth that can transform everything; the experience of the living Christ in the life of the believer.

"Almighty God, who through your only begotten Son Jesus Christ overcame death and opened to us the gate of everlasting life; Grant that we who celebrate with joy the day of our Lord's resurrection may be raised from the death of sin by your life-giving Spirit; through Jesus Christ our Lord who lives and reigns with you and the Holy Spirit, one God, now and for ever." (Prayer Book).

"Ring, joyous bells of Easter, Death hath not conquered Life; Victorious is our risen Lord, And finished all His strife. From Calvary's mount of darkness; Lo starry lilies bloom; For by the cross we conquer, And fearless face the tomb." (M.E. Sangster).

Looking Back and Looking Forward

"..... one thing I do. Forgetting what is behind and straining toward what is ahead. I press on toward the goal to win the prize for which God has called me heavenward in Christ Jesus." - Philippians 3:13, 14.

Among the many imponderables of life there is one certainty - time passes. How to use it wisely and well is the concern of most of us. A looking back at how we spent our time often produces regrets that we did not make better use of it. This dissatisfaction is a proper reaction to what we recall, for to be satisfied with how we live could show insensitivity to the feelings of others; failure to recognise one's own weaknesses; reluctance to acknowledge our indebtedness to God and to other people.

The question we have to ask and answer is - while we move on in time are we moving on in grace and in usefulness as those who are devoted to Christ and committed to His service and the service of others?

The Christian must not be static, standing still, for if his life is not a progression in the knowledge and experience of God it will be a falling away from Him, a following of Christ afar off.

Some of us appear to have reached a comfortable condition in our Christian lives where we have a sense of security in our faith in Christ; a commitment to the church in its work and witness; and a recognition of certain community duties and responsibilities. We have found in our faith a sufficiency for spiritual safety, a comfortable spiritual sit-down.

There is lack of vision, of the sense of deep commitment and real involvement in the practice and outreach of the faith. We should be striving after better things, determining to go on in our spiritual development, growing in grace and in usefulness. The right attitude is to look forward, to go forward for the prize which Paul described as "the high calling of God in Christ Jesus."

The Christian is on a journey. Every victory over self and sin is a spur from which to make progress. Paul was always the constant seeker after larger spiritual experiences. He spoke of forgetting the past, of not living in the past, but learning from it. He would have agreed that "the present is only intelligible in the light of the past." Unfortunately many of us clutter up our minds with what we would be better to forget. A good "forgetery" can be more beneficial than a good memory, for forgetting may be a memory release and not a memory lapse. We must not make a burden of memories which harass and impede us. There is nothing more crippling than recollections of reasons for regret and annoyance.

But while spiritual progress may be affected adversely by upsetting remembrances, it can also be held back by a continuous reflecting on past virtues, pleasures and successes. To go on must mean leaving the sadness and gladness behind and to be ready for what the future holds for us. The main task must be to seek to attain that standard of character and conduct which we have illustrated for us in the life of Jesus. It will be beyond our reach but to be kept in our sights.

To grow in grace is to be done in time honoured ways:

- by prayer - the communing of the soul with God;
- by the Bible - God's ordinary means of conversation with us;
- by the Church - its worship, ministry, teaching, preaching and fellowship.

Spiritual growth will show in the work and worth of the Christian as he lives his life and serves people in the ways of Christ.

A main characteristic of Christianity is its down to earthness, for Christianity is in itself practical. It has no trait more striking than its common sense. And we have the promise that God will give us the strength we need to face whatever life has in store for us, and to accept its challenges in the knowledge that He is with us in them. He said, "I am with you always."

We should remember that the whole of Christianity is comprised in three things, to believe, to love and to obey Jesus. These are things we must be learning and working at all times.

Standing at the Cross

"When they came to the place called the skull, there they crucified Him, along with the criminals - one on His right, the other on His left. Jesus said, 'Father forgive them, for they do not know what they are doing.' And they divided up His clothes by casting lots." Luke 23:33. "And sitting down they watched Him there."

Calvary was where Jesus Christ was crucified by a coaliton of church, state and people. There to be seen was the intoleration of the Pharisees; the exclusiveness of Caiaphas and the priests; the imperial might of Rome and the executive power of Pontius Pilate; the disappointment of the people who expected so much from Him and whose feelings for Him were turned to resentment and abuse. These put Christ on the Cross. And there, too, were the disciple who denied knowing Him and the others who had deserted Him, and the false witnesses who had testified against Him.

Everyone had reason for doing as he did and all of them were guilty much or little for His death. And yet they were not the determining factor in His death, for Jesus went to His death by His own choosing when by standing firm for what He believed He accepted His fate. He had foreseen and foretold how His life would end. As we see Christ on the Cross we recall His words, "The Son of Man came to give His life" and "No man takes (my life) from Me, but I lay it down Myself." "The Son of Man must suffer and be slain." It was the "must" not of constraint but of choice.

Crucifixion was regarded as the most horrific method of capital punishment even in a world accustomed to violence and extreme cruelty. It was shameful and degrading of victims, authorities and spectators. Paul quoting Deuteronomy said "Cursed is everyone that hangs on a tree."

So that when the disciples of Jesus preached about the Cross of Christ they met with the opposition of Jew and Gentile. They had to explain what really happened at Calvary and how the sacrifice of Jesus Christ affects everyone, everywhere and forever. It was to bring God and Man together in that relationship desired by God and needed by people.

"We may not know, we can not tell, what pains He had to bear, but we believe it was for us He hung and suffered there."

Why the Cross? Because by His death on the Cross Jesus affirmed that a power would be released to bring people into a right relationship with God and with one another. In his play "The Trial of Jesus" John Masefield has a scene where the Roman centurion, Longinus, made his report on the crucifixion of Jesus to Pontius Pilate. After the meeting Pilate's wife Procula called him to her room and to her he retold the events of Calvary. When he finished she asked, "Do you think he is dead?" To which he replied, "No, lady, I do not." "Then where is he?" she wondered. Longinus responded, "Let loose in the world, where neither Roman nor Jew can stop his truth."

The people and attitudes which put Christ on the Cross are still around. Evil is constantly at work trying to destroy what is good.

The Cross of Christ reveals the extent of God's love for people. It says that our relationship with God comes from our response to what He has done for us in the Person and Work of Jesus Christ.

> "Could my zeal no respite know, Could my tears for ever flow. All for sin could not atone; Thou must save and Thou alone."

The Cross was not an end but a beginning. The curse of Calvary became a blessing and the gloom of Good Friday was followed by the joy of Easter Day. Christians speak of Christ crucified and risen again. The good news of Jesus Christ is of life. Not Christ is dead; but Christ is alive.

A thought for Easter: the four 'that's'

"I delivered unto you first of all that which I also received." St Paul,
I Corinthians 15.3

St. Paul, in an economical use of words, gives us the core of what he calls his "received gospel." He does it in four short precise statements - "that He died; that He was buried; that He was raised; and that He was seen ......!"

The gospel is the good news of Jesus Christ and Paul heard it from His disciples who were witnesses to the person and power of Jesus.

The experience of Paul is that of every Christian for the Christian faith is passed on person to person, generation to generation. The place and purpose of the church is to be the repository for and the transmitter of the gospel. It does that by public worship, with its prayers, scriptures, sacraments and songs; its preaching, teaching, and outreach to people with that message. The gospel is summed up in the statement, "Christianity is Christ," He is the pivotal person, the focus of the faith.

Paul's thesis is that everything important in life is available to people by Him and through Him. He is the God-provided means by which God shows Himself as a Person to people. Faith in Him, and commitment to Him, make for an essential relationship with God, and a proper, beneficial, relationship people with people.

There is never any need to search for the evidence of the value of the faith for people are everywhere who find their lives enhanced and enriched by their faith in Jesus Christ. It is not only meaningful but integral to their living. It gives strength to the weak, hope to the fearful and peace of mind to the perplexed. It is for many the reason for living, that which makes sense of their lives, to make them live selflessly for God and people.

The received gospel of Paul was of crucial importance to him as it is, and has been, to Christians all the time and everywhere, but the faith can be to some acceptance of its truth but with little pressure on them to live it out in their lives. Their inertia accounts for the disinterest of others in the relevance of the faith to them.

They do not give the impression that the faith matters to them and so their lives are no persuasion on others to seek a faith that appears to be of little consequence to those who claim it. Paul's emphasis was on the death and resurrection of Jesus. Jesus

Christ, risen from the dead, was his constant theme as it was the main message of the disciples and those near to Him in the days of His flesh.

The early church had the one subject - Jesus, crucified and alive again. The church's commission remains the same, to preach, teach and live out the great fundamentals of the faith. And the fundamentals include this concentration of St. Paul - his four thats, the church's mission has four goals:

- to proclaim the good news of Jesus Christ;
- to teach and nurture new believers;
- to respond positively to human need;
- to seek to change what is unjust in society.

The programme is clear and the carrying out of it is dependent on the strength of the believers, individually and collectively in their commitment to Christ and their certainty that the good news of Jesus Christ is the best news for human kind all the time and everywhere.

St. Patrick:
the real Patron Saint revealed

St. Patrick's Day March 17, with its concentration on Ireland and the Irish and its celebrations in music and song, parades and parties, has long been the most popular day of the year for many more than the Irish. It has been said with more than a little accuracy that all in New York are Irishmen on St. Patrick's Day with the green of the Emerald Isle the colouring for everything.

That the day is well known everywhere does not mean that Patrick is any more than a name to very many; and that could apply to Ireland too. People need to be reminded or told that the patron saint of Ireland was a Christian preacher, teacher and writer whose life and work had such an effect on his time and thereafter that he is to be seen as the pivotal person in the beginnings, and development of Christianity in Ireland. As with historical figures generally much has been written about St. Patrick.

BACKGROUND

When the man speaks for himself we learn some things about him. He does that in two writings - his "Confession" and "The Letter to Coroticus", in five sayings in the book of Armagh and the hymn, "The Breastplate" which has been attributed to him. He tells us he was a Roman Briton from Bonnaven Taberniae. The location of which has been set in Scotland, near Dumbarton on the River Clyde and in North Wales near Milford and we are left with these uncertain choices. His father was Calpurnius, a farmer and deacon of his church and his grandfather was Potitus, a priest. Captured and taken as a slave to Ireland he served a chieftain, Milchu, as a swineherd and cattle drover for six years on Slemish Mountain in Co. Antrim. In his captivity Patrick came to see his dire straits as a punishment for his neglect of God. He described in his Confession how he "earnestly sought God and then I found Him."

TRAINING

After he escaped from his captivity there followed the "Silent Years" in which at home he worked and trained to be a minister of the Gospel. In a time of religious awakening in Europe Patrick studied in Gaul, France, where his mentor was Germanus, the Bishop of Auxerre, and perhaps in Rome. It was in these Silent Years that he had a Paul-like vision of one Victorious bearing letters and one "The Voice of the Irish." As he took the letter he "heard the voice of those who lived beside the wood Foclut near the Western sea." Responding to the call to "come over and help us" he returned to Ireland, having been consecrated a bishop by Germanus. The year was 432 and by his leadership there began the growth and development of the Celtic church. An early covert was the chieftain, Dichu, who gave him a site at Saul, Co. Down, where his first church, "Patrick's Barn" was built. From that beginning there were churches to follow in several places as Patrick and his Christians converted people from paganism. And these Celtic Christians were to take the faith to Britain and Europe with incredible results in the spread of Christianity. Whatever historians say about Patrick and Celtic Christianity his writings are Bible-based - the scriptures are quoted extensively - and his preaching and teaching was Christ centred and people orientated.

PRACTICE

The legacy of St. Patrick is a Christianity free from the disunities and distresses that have adversely affected it in Ireland for many centuries. A cure for the ills, divisions and disturbances of today would be in return to the emphases of St. Patrick - the fundamentals of Christian belief and the primary purpose of the churches and Christians to bring people to faith in Christ to enjoy the benefits of the Gospel.

Denominational claims on Patrick mean little when what is important is that the man be seen for what he was - a pattern Christian whose life and work should be a persuasion on Christians everywhere to be as he was in his commitment and witness to Christ and in his service for people. If that thought is not lost in the festivities of St. Patrick's Day there is gain for those who participate in them.

The realities of Harvest

Jesus said, "The kingdom of God is like this. A man scatters seed on the land; he goes to bed at night and gets up in the morning, and the seed sprouts and grows – how, he does not know. The ground produces a crop by itself, first, the blade, then the ear, then full-grown corn in the ear; but as soon as the crop is ripe, he sets to work with the sickle because the harvest-time has come."

Harvest thanksgiving services to many people are the most popular services of their churches. Their involvement in them is at once inspirational and practical. The specially prepared music and song; the decorated church with its beautiful flowers, plants and edible fruit and vegetables, the aesthetic and the earthy, reminders of the intrinsic worth of harvest and the reason for thankfulness that we live where there is a plentiful harvest. And to God we pray, "as You have given us the knowledge to produce plenty, so give us the will to bring it within the reach of others."

In the harvest we see God and man working productively together.

"Back of the loaf is the snowy flour. Back of the flour is the mill. Back of the mill are the wind and the shower. And the sun and the Father's will."

Jesus used nature to remind people that their dependence should be in God. He taught many lessons which had their illustrations in the countryside.

"He spoke of lilies, vines and corn. The sparrow and the raven, and words so natural and yet so wise where on men's hearts engraven, and yeast and bread and flax and cloth. And eggs and fish and candles. See how the most familiar world. He most divinely handles."

Jesus saw life as co-operation between God and people. We are constantly amazed at the ingenuity of farmers and scientists whose knowledge and skills contribute so much to the high standards in agriculture, horticulture, animal husbandry, food production and processing of the various products familiar to us, but the experts have their limitations. They do what they can and nature does the rest.

Jesus used this little story to say things about trust and gratitude. He said the farmer sowed his seed and then went home to sleep. He did what had to be done and left the rest to God. Experience had taught him that what he sowed would come to harvest. If he hadn't had that confidence he wouldn't have turned a furrow or sown a seed. The thought of harvest caused one man to say, "What I have seen induces me to trust God for what I have not seen."

Jesus spoke of gratitude, trust and confidence, "First the blade, then the year after that the full corn in the ear." Harvest is reaped after months of working and waiting. Life often demands a struggle to obtain the desired results. We are thankful that we have a way of life so different and so much better than what is to be found in many parts of the world. And we are reminded that it was our people's sense of justice and decency which produced our caring society. That is the reason why, at our best and most unselfish, we respond positively to the calls of despair from those in need elsewhere in the world.

A theme of harvest thanksgiving must be that the worship of God has the practical implication that the worshipper will be copiers of Christ in compassion and care for other people.

Our thanksgiving for the benefits we enjoy, if it is meaningful, will show in how we treat others. The spirit of harvest thanksgiving must not be an occasional but a continuing exercise in our lives. It must be purposeful in a selflessness Christ-like in its concern for people.

"Giving is living," the angel said, "So feed the hungry sweet charity's bread". "And Must I keep giving and giving again?" "Oh, no." said the angel piercing me through, "Just give 'til the Master stops giving to you."

The Christian is encouraged to have and to develop that spirit of thanksgiving which is effective in lifting the hearts and minds of people. There is always the persuasion of Scripture, "in everything give thanks," "be thankful for small mercies," and "be thankful always."

In a word or two harvest has to do with thanksgiving and giving.

Section Four:

Issues for the Churches and Christians today

Think of these things

Efforts are contstanly being made "to make church services more attractive to those who attend them". A laudable exercise, of course, but how to produce services that are appealing to more than the relatively small percentage of the population who attend them is the perennial question.

Those churches which have a higher than average number of satisfied members appear to provide the elements in music, song and sermon which make their services meaningful and enjoyable. There is acceptance of form and format and participation and satisfaction in them. The congregation is emotionally involved readily accepting that stated aims and objectives of the church service. There is anticipation that what is projected will happen and its results will be seen.

The elements in the service are worship - prayer and praise; teaching - by scriptures and sermon; emphasis on personal response to what is being said and heard. A feature in these services is the certainty that what is happening is as God wills it. There is total reliance on the veracity and value of the scriptures and a high valuation on preaching. There is also a strong sense of fellowship, a togetherness in common cause which is contagious.

This is the case in some churches and they point up the difference between them and other often older, so-called main churches. The elements may not be dissimilar. The differences are in the emphasis and valuations on what is important and more important. The quality of devotion may not be different but where in the one there is certainty, spontaneity and expectation, the other is subdued, meditative and placid.

These different attitudes are easily recognised and the swift conclusion is that satisfaction in worship is not in the similarities but in the differences. That may account for the proliferation of churches, fellowships and meeting places in the search for the sometimes elusive spiritual harbour.

The struggle of many churches is to provide forms of service which meet the needs of their members and are attractive to others. No longer are church leaders and people satisfied with what their fathers found sufficient in worship. No longer, because of experimentation, can we be assured that a service will be ordered as formerly; that the published liturgy of the church, where there is one, will be used.

Inevitably, changes meant to meet the wishes of minister and members or to affect the thinking of unattached people, have caused some embarrassement, for there are always those who resist change. They are not convinved that the changes will be effective in deepening the spiritual life of the church or in persuading others to join with them.

Because the faith is presented to people the pressure is always on the Christian to make effort to bring others to faith in Christ. Whatever is done in the attempt to make church services and the presentation of the faith more acceptable it must not change for change sake. That could have the effect of reducing rather than enlarging church attendances.

It must be added that the most public way to show that the Christian faith has meaning for us is by our attendance at the public worship of the church. It says - "I believe in God ...." as clearly as the words of the confessions of the faith. It is a necessity for the development of the Christian life. John Wesley said "There is no such thing as a solitary Christian."

Why the Church?

"And he is the head of the body, the Church: who is the beginning, the first born from the dead, that in all things he might have the pre-eminence."
Colossians 1:18.

Time was when people spoke of "our church", "your church", "the church," in explanation and commendation. The words are still used, but much less frequently, for to very many, religion and the church is not what matters to them. Their focus in our largely secularised society is on the material; and personal and familial relationships, which can do without the extras religion offers them.

A fair generalisation, perhaps, but with many there is the heritage of bits and pieces of the Christian faith learned in childhood, and kept in cache to be used for comfort and hope, when more than the secular is required to meet a need. The continued use of the church by those with little or no attachment to it is witness to that. And the church responds in the hope that by the services it provides these people will come to faith in Christ.

Time is when people ask "Why the church?" and in their attitudes show indifference, refusal to see value in it for them. The cynic saying that this is because the church is no longer of interest to people, adds that the church is no longer interested in people. If the prognosis is true it is a most serious indictment of the church. The signs of an unattractive, disinterested, church are lack of fellowship, of care and concern member for member, and a loss of commitment to the place and purpose of the church in the plan of God for people. Its primary task is to bring people to faith in Christ, "to seek and to save the lost."

The church of today and yesterday are markedly different in emphases and attitudes. Worship modes are more liberal; pastoral visitation less practised; organisations absent or little valued. Changes have come by pressures in a society breaking from the past and embracing new means of communication common in it. How these are used and to what advantage, is the question confronting the church?

Changes are necessary, of course, in the worship, work and witness of the church. They are best when the old ways are valued. To discard the old is a nonsense for what is most valuable, and memorable, in human thought and action is timeless, forever relevant.

There is a problem when changes are forced against the wishes of those who find them an intrusion on the forms and ceremonies which distinguish their church from others. Dr. Billy Graham encourages thought on the subject when he says:

"There is a kind of unity in diversity, a unity compatible with variety, and it is this pattern which Christ lays down for the church." Another added, *"Stop confining Christ to the church, start taking Him to a world that needs hope and salvation."*

F.W. Boreham, while speaking of himself and his ministry, described the task of the church: "to proclaim the magnificent virtues of the Christian gospel - with absolute certainty, and with unwavering confidence about the sin of man, the cross of Christ ..... Because there is nothing else to be said."

When we think of the strengths and weaknesses of the church we realise that strength comes with action, success by work, weakness is failure. It is to recognise that a lazy, indolent church tends to uncertainty and inaction while an earnest busy church, facing up to the problems in society, sin, misery, inequality and injustice, grows stronger in faith and fellowship. Whatever is said about changes in the church: "Neither a person, nor a church, nor a nation, can live on the achievements of the past."

Angus McVicar, a modern prophet warns:

"If Christ's message is eroded by inaction then the whole structure of our civilisation will tumble back and down into a pagan chaos."

Billy Graham says it too: *"Unless men of purpose, integrity and faith stand together in unswerving loyalty to Jesus Christ the future of the world is bleak indeed."*

Say something: have something to say

"When Samuel spoke all Israel listened". 1 Samuel 3:23.

Samuel of the Old Testament earned a proud reputation as judge and ruler in Israel for he was an honest man whose conduct and way of life was beyond reproach. He was the man he was because as a man of God he took his faith seriously. He owed character-making influences to his mother, Hannah, who dedicated him to the service of God as her response in gratitude for the gift of a son; to growing up in the Temple, taught by the priests, closeted where the things of God filled their minds. He gained much from these devout and disciplined people.

There are those who speak of their Godly parents and good Christian homes even when they have long since ceased to practice the faith of their childhood and give little or no credence to their Christian heritage. Many believers, however, gladly admit their indebtedness to parents, family, teachers, church and friends who helped them make the Christian faith their own and to live by it.

There is always this dilemma - the influence of parents, home, family, friends, effective in the moulding of character and in setting good and proper patterns in behaviour, and the rejection by so many of a similar upbringing and that even when for some it remains something to turn to for comfort and consolation in the crisis times in their lives. These different responses have much to do with personality and individuality and influences which affect their thinking and living; attitudes, responses and objectives that come out of their experiences of life as they live it.

There are Christians whose faith is their received and acknowledged inheritance. They travel easy, satisfied with who and what they are, and their loyalty, devotion and generousity to their church guarantees its existence and continuing usefulness as the fellowship of the faithful in that place. Totally dependable they can be inward-thinking, lacking in their Christian commitment to be outgoing to others to serve them and to win them for Christ. Enthusiasts who take seriously the command of Jesus to bring others to Him are not encouraged when how they speak and act differs from the usual practices of their church.

There is evidence, however, that churches are more readily meeting their responsibility to reach out to people with the good news of Jesus Christ, to convince them of their need of Him in their lives. Efforts are being made to equip members to do what is required of them in a task to which Christ has committed every Christian.

Clergy and leaders in the churches have the responsibility of encouraging their members to do their duty to God and other people with whom they have contact and in whatever capacity. Samuel had to do that and because he set a good example to the people when he spoke everyone listened. And he spoke plainly and precisely on duties and responsibilities so that none would misunderstand him. It is essential that Christian leaders speak as Samuel did forthrightly and sensitively to people who live often in complex situations and difficult environments.

The pressure on church and people is to be involved in whatever effects people to do what should be done to improve society. Everything that troubles the citizen should concern the church. It is to its credit that it often makes a large contribution to the betterment of the communities it serves. It has a gospel to proclaim and it provides the motivation for positive responses to those in need of help in their lives, whether admitted or denied.

The church is at its best when it is out in the world with its plea to people to have faith in God; when it is feeding the hungry, clothing the naked, healing the sick and educating the illiterate, when it is championing the causes of the poor and oppressed and opposing political systems and tyrannies which belittle, injure and destroy people.

The church is most ineffective when it is inward-looking, concentrating only on doctrines, liturgies and structures to the exclusion of more important and pressing matters; when it loses sight of its destiny as the one organisation which is not for itself but for others.

The church ought not to be a holy huddle, a select circle of the like-minded but a home for everyone who admits his need of God and comes to Him in faith and trust. It is the people of God who share in the worship of God, recognise their indebtedness to Christ and determine to serve Him and their fellow men as the Holy Spirit equips and enables them.

The Faith and the Fight Back

"Don't let the world around you squeeze you into its own mould, but let God remould your minds from within, so that you may prove in practice that the plan of God for you is good, meets all His demands and moves towards the goal of true maturity."
"Don't allow yourself to be overpowered with evil. Take the offensive - overpower evil with good." Romans 12:2 and 21. (JBP)

The onward march of secularism and the "retreat" from Christianity elicits the question - what if the faith is lost to the Western world, and that which has inspired millions to face life responsibility and death fearlessly is gone? The response must be to think of what such a loss would mean to people whose civilisation has been built on Christian principles with their high valuation on the human personality and community, motivated by ideals which persuade them to strive to reach standards of behaviour that make us good citizens valueing ourselves and respecting one another.

It would be to lose the motives, restraints and incentives the faith supplies and which saves society from degenerating into a state of lawlessness, violence, inhumanity and indecency.

The faith provides solidity and decency where Christians affect the thinking and doing of people whose aspiration is to make a good, fair, just and humane society. We are well acquainted with the vices of a debased humanity - selfishness, avarice, irresponsible wealth and the neglected poor who suffer disadvantages from childhood to old age.

The absence of church people from the positions of power and influence they had in education and the social services has affected the country positively and negatively. Positively in that the state's much greater involvement in both has provided better facilities in buildings, facilities, and equipment. Negatively in that the formerly close contact of church to children and all age adults has been weakened, even minimised.

There are once strong youth organisations with their influence on the lives of many people, but secularism and materialism are the main causes of the weaknesses of the churches.

The situation means that the church has to strive much harder to change trends antagonistic or indifferent to it. It must do that for the apparent acceptance by many

Christians of the present position is defeatist and disabling of the presence and purpose of the church. It is the attitude that dissuades people from turning to Christ and is a denial of its commission which is to make Christians.

The unchanging single emphasis of the Christian faith is the worth and work of Jesus Christ as the Lord and Saviour of people. Some will criticise, depreciate, withstand Him but they must not ignore Him for He is always here. He never goes away. He continues to change the lives of people to make them, and even the castaways of society, into exemplary citizens and good people. A personal, positive, commitment to Christ is the most important and beneficial deliberate decision a person can make in life.

We live in a society which takes religious ideas and robs them of their religious content, but the ideas are only workable properly in their Christian context. It is the task of the church to ensure that the Christian voice is heard in everything that matters to people.

The message is Jesus Christ, the messengers Christians, the task to ensure that the benefits of the faith are known to everyone. To persuade others to turn to Christ for in Him is the answer to the needs of people everywhere.

They do that by Christ-taught character and conduct in the assurance that He is with them in what they say and do for Him.

Churches – the same only different

The forms of worship in the Protestant churches, the attitudes and responses of worshippers, the emphases on prayer, Bible reading and preaching are "the same only different." The same in their devotion, exhortation, petition and intercession, whether the form is liturgical, of set order, or spontaneous and momentary. Different in how they express themselves as churches in a society increasingly secularistic and irreligious.

There is the solidity, predictability, of the older churches which have patterns of behaviour in faith and practice, proven by experience and acceptable as proper and pertinent in their witness to Christ. A changelessness that evokes loyalty in their people who have a sense of history, and of gratitude for a heritage to be passed on to their children and their children's children.

They teach the faith conscientiously in the ways they receive it from parents, teachers and preachers while leaving the reception of it to the person to whom it is addressed. There is little or no persuasion or pressure on anyone who hears it. He knows where the church stands on belief and behaviour and he responds as he pleases. There is the quiet, comfortable, contentment of the 'main' churches.

We generalise, of course, some of them are outgoing, adventurous, in their approach to people and it shows in their worship and work in the community.

They involve themselves in activities that could be described as rescuing people from their sins and weaknesses and encouraging them to turn to Christ for strength and purpose in their lives.

While these attitudes are shared by the Protestant churches there is a gulf fixed between them. That is best illustrated by comparisons made between the main, older, churches and the younger churches in this society. Where the older are usually introverted, with a concentration on their own people, the younger are extroverted with an outreach to "all sorts and conditions of men".

To attend the services of the churches is to be made aware of the differences in people, their attitudes and appearances. There remains a Sunday-go-to-meeting look that is shared, but styles of dress and types of people are different. There is the feeling that those who are deeply committed to the one will not be found in membership of the other. Certainly not until there has been a conversion experience. When that happens it is often from the older to the younger churches. Many of the churches in the older denominations are finding it hard to maintain their strengths. Losses by natural causes are not being filled by new people, for in our secularised society very many young people, whose parents are committed church members, think religion undesirable and unnecessary, to them. Whereas in the younger churches there is growth, phenomenal in some cases, and that of all ages and the young markedly.

Studies have been made on the reasons for a situation that is becoming more and more apparent, and their findings are worth examining. The first question has to be why is there stalemate on the one hand and growth on the other. It would appear to some that the answer lies in the different emphases on the fundamentals of the faith. Where the older are agreeable to have, and to allow, personal and preferential interpretations of scripture, creeds and doctrinal statements, the younger are adamant on the necessity of believing in and holding on to the accuracy of scripture, the acceptance of the reality of the Virgin Birth, the resurrection and divinity of Jesus Christ. The liberalism of the older churches, and the questioning of these beliefs, makes the differences, older and younger, divisive and with consequences which must account to an extent, for the weaknesses from the uncertainties of the one and the strength from the certainties of the other.

We live in a society of contradictions, for while there are many who find they can live without a religious faith, there are those who want the dogmatism, fundamentalism, of a Christianity which has the truth and is not to be doubted or doctored. Because these are the deliberate choices of people we accept their effects on a Protestantism which is individualistic, separative, and sometimes competitive with unhappy consequences.

The differences between some older and younger churches are to be found in their attitudes to ministry. While they are alike in their high valuation on ministry their requirements for it are dissimilar in that the older churches expect academic qualifications from their ministers, pastors in some younger churches are chosen with or without such distinctions. Previous experience of life, and of church worth and witness, are regarded as first essentials. Because ministers and pastors, whatever their academic status, have been faithful and fruitful in their ministries there is no one way that is the only way.

A difference, too, could be their attitudes to pastoral ministry and Christian fellowship. Older churches which had a reputation for their valuation on these appear now to put less value on house to house visiting and person to person contact in the homes of the people. Younger churches have a concentration on this so that the sense of belonging, of being a member of the family of the Church is a felt experience to them and a source of comfort and pleasure, especially to those who would be lonely and alone without that care and attention.

And language distinguishes the churches. The use of scriptural words and phrases by the younger, seldom heard in the older such as saved, born-again filled with the Spirit. Words that are in the everyday vocabulary of those of the younger churches. They are used in what is declared to be the supreme task of the church, winning souls for Christ. There is the expectation that by the preaching of the Word and the prayers and persuasion by word and example of the faithful, souls will be saved.

The strong sense of the effects of evangelism apparent in younger churches is not obvious in the older churches. It was not always so.

The Church and Youth

"Delight in your boyhood, young man, make the most of the days of your youth; let your heart and your eyes show you the way; but remember for all these things God will call you to account. Remember your creator in the days of your youth." Ecclesiastes 11.9: 12.1

The "youth problem" has been with the churches for a long time. How to keep the young in or to bring them into the church remains a matter of constant concern.

There have been many investigations into the attitudes of young people to religion, and special efforts made to have them accept the claim of Christ and the Christian faith to be the answer to the fundamental needs of people for a happy, useful and fulfilled life.

Churches have examined themselves in the attempt to ensure that they are relevant to young people. This has meant attention being given to the services of the church. It has brought forms of worship in addition to or in place of those used in little altered form for centuries. The intention has been to meet the needs of the young for the free and easy worship and greater and more varied use of music.

The results have been varied and revealing. They have produced the expected reaction from those who are satisfied with that to which they are accustomed, uncomplimentary comments, sometimes, more seriously, resistance to the churches and absence from church. There is a dilemma - get the young in by changes and lose others because of them.

How to meet the different responses of people and to gain new members while not losing old ones, is the question to be answered in many churches. There is the additional complication that there are young folk who prefer the old to the new. They like the dignity and discipline of well ordered, precise and published forms of common prayer for public worship.

There has been a proliferation of groups, and events catering for young people, well supported and much enjoyed by those who participate in them. There is evidence that these young people benefit from such experiences and by them are brought closer into the life of their church, but there are many more who are not interested in such happenings. And it is they the churches have to influence if their futures are to be secured.

It is easy to describe the situation of the church and youth. How to tackle the problem effectively is the question awaiting answers. We have none except to post the reminder that the churches in paying particular attention to their young people must be welcoming and appreciative of them.

A strong sense of family which shows in concern for them is most important. Too often young people have felt uncomfortable in church and especially in these days when their number is small in congregation of the middle and old aged. Projects to help young people to live happy and healthy lives are to be commended.

The trials, tribulations and temptations they face were unknown to past generations. Efforts being made by churches to deal with the young holistically, to cater for their spiritual, mental and physical needs is especially deserving of support. The use of trained people in specialist posts must do much to make us hopeful of their success. History is often cyclical. When the youth problem was recognised in the late 19th and early 20th centuries organisations were founded to win and hold young people for Christ and the church - the Girls Friendly Society in 1875, the Boys' Brigade in 1883, the Boy Scouts in 1907, the Girl Guides in 1910 and youth clubs followed quickly.

These were programmes of the churches to give to the young, in the setting of the church, the opportunity to enjoy Christian fellowship and to know and to value Christian teaching on life, liberty and the pursuit of happiness. The organisations were aids towards knowing, worshipping and serving the Lord and Saviour, Jesus Christ.

Their successes were remarkable and their good work continues, albeit nowadays when organisations are disregarded generally and the uniformed ones particularly. A repeat of these successes of other days by different methods would go far to rejuvenate the churches.

Religion – more or less

To some the evidence that many people in Britain prefer secularism/materialism to Christian faith and morality is everywhere and all the time in the decline of religion. The refusal to see it as an essential to life in a society, self centred, self sufficient, self controlled and with the philosophy that whatever makes people happy has to be permissible and acceptable. The reality is that in England fewer than nine per cent regularly attend a church service.

To others the state of religion is different. They do not question the attendance figures of the Church of England, and they recognise that the Roman Catholic Church is affected by the drop in numbers attending masses.

They point up causes for such a situation - the confusion in the Church of England on what it believes and teaches about God, people and human relationships; and in the Roman Catholic Church demoralised by child abuse and the refusal to release its priesthood from the vow of celibacy.

In spite of this evidence most people are influenced and affected by the Christian faith and show their indebtedness to it by living their lives on principles, that if not exclusively Christian in origin, are for them their heritage from Christianity. And they show their preference for the Christian standards of conduct in their choice of schools for their children. Church schools are preferred, not just because they get good examination results but that in them there is order and discipline needful in a society suffering from the lack of them. A society in a state of worry and uncertainty about how to cope with many problems and especially those caused by drink and drug abuse and escalating crime.

Whatever contributions are made by others, Christians are deeply involved in the fight against whatever threatens and destroys the lives of people. They have answers to questions on how people should live before God, for themselves and with other people.

The charge is made that the churches are not speaking up to be heard in attacks on the evils in their society; that there is a liberalism in the churches which makes lesser standards acceptable and there is accommodation for what was regarded as alien to beliefs and practices seen to be integral to Christian faith and practice.

This questioning of theological, doctrinal, sociological and historical articles of the faith has caused some to leave them for others certain in what they believe and whose members practice their faith in patterns of behaviour distinctive, recognisably different, from what is allowable in them.

Another reality then is the increasing strength and growth of evangelical churches in England - they are virile and active in the older denominations - and fellowships, where the many and not the few congregate to worship God, join in the fellowship of shared faith; and in encouraging people to believe as they do by persuading them to come and hear the Gospel read and preached or by bringing it to them where they are.

You may ask what of this is applicable to Northern Ireland. Great Britain and Northern Ireland are not the same in their attitudes to religion. Here there is a higher percentage of church attenders - though in some urban areas only minimally higher - and much more interest in the churches and their activities. Many are sufficiently of the church to use its services when they are desirable for specific purposes. But that said the attitudes of many people to religion is similar to the rest of the United Kingdom. The problems are the same for what has to be faced in Great Britain must be confronted in Northern Ireland.

What we think to be needed, there and here, is the realisation that the Christian faith has the answers to the ills and problems of life; that it is the duty of Christians to ensure that people hear that message loud and clear, for the prime purpose of Christianity is to give a meaning to living, a purpose for life and a way of life.

Music and Song

"Express your joy in singing among yourselves psalms and hymns and spiritual songs, making music in your hearts for the ears of God."
Ephesians 5:19

Integral to the services of the Christian church is the worship of God, and the ministry of the Word and the Sacrament. Whether the services are formal, liturgical or spontaneous, extemporary, these are essential to them.

Integral, too, to the services of the church are its psalms, hymns, spiritual songs and instrumental music. Varied in form, style, quality and quantity they play a large part in the public worship of Christians. In many churches their role is becoming more and more apparent and significant.

There is the recognition that most people have an inbuilt love of music and song, that in them their feelings and emotions are most adequately expressed. It is much easier to be with others in music and song than to join them in prayers, sermons and ceremonies in church. This because people often "speak with the head and sing with the heart."

Even those with a minimal interest in religion find it easy to use the church's music and song in the crises of their lives. They are the natural expression of feelings and emotions; joy and sorrow; hope and expectation; devotion and commitment.

Christian enthusiasm is most readily expressed in music and song; music beyond words and words singable and meaningful. "A song will outlive all sermons in the memory."

There is always need for balance in the services of the church, the parts are dependent on one another, enhancing one another. The blend of prayer and praise, scripture and sermon is necessary when there is devotion to God in worship and a receptive sharing in the learning process by scripture and sermon by the people of God.

Charles Kingsley has a warning for anyone who elevates singing over everything else: "Do not fancy, as too many do, that thou canst praise God by singing hymns to Him in church once a week and disobeying Him all the week long. He asks of thee works as well as words; and more. He asks of works first and words after."

The warning noted there is reason to pay compliment to those whose music and song contributes so much to the deepening of the spiritual lives of believers and for bringing others to faith in Christ. There is "reward" for the composers and authors whose works receive the highest commendation, constant use. Some of them are well-known names whose lives have inspired us for the depth of their commitment to Christ and the variety of their experiences before and after the faith caught hold of them.

They were men and women inspired to say in music and song what was necessary to speak for God to people and people to God. "Glorious the song, when God is the theme."

As we think of the use of music and song we may show preferences, for the quality and quantity is variable in the extreme. Describe it as you will the choices are numerous and yet there is much music and song which have universal approval and frequent use.

We have preferences in our choices of what we hear and sing in church. We want to easily recognise what is being played or sung. We have sympathy for someone who hoped that God knew what a soloist was singing for he did not.

It must be the essence of good music and song that there be no need for anyone to complain about its audibilty, clarity and intelligibility. Having said this we have to add that everyone should be encouraged to sing in the congregation. Most people can sing. Few things are more impressive about church than Christians singing together in response to the psalmist, "Let everything that hath breath praise the Lord."

The accessible master and the acceptable message

"The common people heard him gladly". Mark 12:37.

"God must love the common people He made so many of them," said Abraham Lincoln. It was the common people who responded to Jesus and his message of love - of God for them and them for one another. He persuaded them to recognise their need of God and their dependence on Him for purpose, and quality in their lives; and on other people to live usefully and unselfishly together.

Common people have been criticised for their innocence, ignorance and lack of initiative; regarded contemptuously by "superior people". There have been times when despised, powerless people were forced to rise up against those who misruled and devalued them. Some of these uprisings had the results the people wanted but too often the replacement of an evil regime was by another no less oppressive.

Only when the common people are treated impartially, honestly and decently can a society be regarded with respect. The common people are the real wealth of any country.

They were at their wisest and most discerning when they gave Jesus a ready hearing, unlike the religious men, politicians and intelligencia who scorned Him. Many of them realised the truth in what He said and some of them were to learn from Him, be healed by Him, to find peace and contentment in their lives as His people. Others, manipulated by His enemies, screamed for His death. They believed the unbelievable about Him and were shamed by what was done to Him.

Mark says: "The common people heard Him". He invited everybody to listen to what He had wanted to tell them. That was unusual when teachers were most selective in those they invited to hear Him. Horace the Roman poet, said, "I hate the vulgar crowd and told them at a distance" and Plato the Greek philosopher disregarded the common people utterly.

Snobbery, whether intellectual, racial or classist is always selective and exclusive. It has never been unknown among Christians. It exists still as a barrier to the outreach of the church to the common people. The accessibility of Jesus is in contrast to the exclusiveness of some who call themselves Christians. He is always the welcoming Christ.

Mark adds, "The common people heard Him gladly". What He told them made them happy. He spoke to their needs and aspirations in everyday settings with conviction and certainty. He was very different from the preachers and teachers who lacked sincerity and were unsure of their message. He talked sense in easily understandable language and He did it sensitively and respectfully. The pattern Jesus set in his approach to people remains the way Christians ought to conduct themselves if they would fulfil their obligation to bring others to faith in God.

The first disciples of Jesus were common people who heard Him gladly and followed Him selflessly, courageously and joyfully. They found their satisfaction in Him and in their service for Him and other people.

The hymn writer echoed this sentiment when he penned:-

> *"O Christ, in Thee my soul hath found,*
> *And found in Thee alone,*
> *the peace, the joy, I sought so long,*
> *The bliss till now unknown.*

The hymn in the Church Hymnary 699 (Church Of Ireland) has the chorus:-

> *"Now none but Christ can satisfy,*
> *None other name for me.*
> *There's love, and life, and lasting joy,*
> *Lord Jesus, found in Thee".*

The task of the church today is to persuade the people of their need to hear Jesus and to respond positively to Him for it is by faith in Him and acceptance of his standards of behaviour that they can live useful and happy lives.